Preparing for

SUNDAYS AND FEAST DAYS— CYCLE A

Daniel Donovan

PAULIST PRESS
New York/Mahwah

Copyright © 1995
by Daniel Donovan

All rights reserved. No part of this book may be reproduced or transmitted in any form or by any means, electronic or mechanical, including photocopying, recording or by any information storage and retrieval system without permission in writing from the Publisher.

Library of Congress Cataloging-in-Publication Data

(Revised for vol. 1)

Donovan, Daniel, 1937-
    Preparing for worship.

    Contents: [1] Cycle A—[2] Cycle B—[3] Cycle C. 1.
    Bible—Liturgical lessons, English. 2. Church year meditations. I. Title.
BX2170.C55D625   1993   242´.3   93-13704
ISBN 0-8091-3571-X

Published by Paulist Press
997 Macarthur Boulevard
Mahwah, N.J. 07430

Printed and bound in the United States of America

Contents

FOR NOREEN, DAVID
AND CATHERINE

"Qu'est-ce que cela fait? Tout est grâce."
("What does that matter? Everything is grace.")

Journal d'un curé de campagne
Georges Bernanos

Introduction

In spite of changing liturgical and cultural patterns, the Sunday eucharist remains for most Christians a defining and nourishing moment in their religious life. In gathering for its celebration they realize again that they belong to a community of faith, a community whose identity is rooted in the life and teaching of Jesus and whose spiritual vitality is dependent on the presence to it of his Spirit.

The eucharistic liturgy is made up of two main parts: the first includes readings from the scriptures, a homily, and prayers; the second recalls within the form of a solemn prayer of praise and thanksgiving what Jesus said over the bread and wine as he distributed them to his disciples at the last supper. The word "eucharist" in its original Greek means literally thanksgiving. It is used both of the great prayer that begins with the invitation of the priest to the people to lift up their hearts and to give thanks to God, and of the Sunday service as a whole, including word and sacrament.

By the early second century the eucharist had taken on the basic form that we know today. The memorial of the last supper, originally celebrated in the context of an evening meal, had become self-standing and was united to a pattern of prayers, readings from the Bible and a homily or sermon that was molded on the traditional service of the Jewish synagogue. This new liturgy was celebrated on Sunday morning, a day that was precious to believers as the day on which Jesus had been raised from the dead. They called it both the first and the eighth day of the week and thought of it as marking the beginning of a new creation.

One of the goals of the renewal of the eucharistic liturgy that received such an impetus from Vatican II (1962-65) was to make its twofold structure more evident. The rites were simplified and the texts were translated into the various languages of the different Catholic communities around the world. A heightened emphasis was given to the scripture readings and to the homily, and a place was created for our present prayers of the faithful.

In order that believers would be exposed to more of the Bible than in the past, a three year cycle of readings for the Sunday liturgy was introduced. Known by the first three letters of the alphabet, the feature that most clearly distinguishes them from one another is the particular gospel that is read on what are called the ordinary Sundays of the year. Matthew, Mark, and Luke are assigned for years A, B, and C, respectively. The gospel of John tends to be used on certain Sundays of Lent and during the Easter Season in all three cycles.

The standard pattern calls for three scriptural readings on Sundays and major feast days. The first of the three is ordinarily taken from one or other of the books of that part of the Bible which Christians share with Jews and which we call the Old Testament. It is almost always chosen because it has some more or less obvious connection with the gospel for that day. The second reading is from a letter of Paul or from one of the other New Testament writings other than the gospels. The practice here is to use readings from a single book over a period of several weeks. Although the second reading sometimes contains themes related to those suggested by the gospel, it is often not the case. This practice has both disadvantages and advantages. While it undermines to some degree the unity of individual liturgies, it does allow people to develop some sense of the distinctive message of the different New Testament writings.

If Sunday and the eucharist together represent a focus for the religious experience of many Catholics, the rhythm of the liturgical year also plays its part. Christians inherited from Judaism a sense of the importance of the yearly celebration of fundamental religious events and realities. For Jews there was no more important a moment in their year than Passover, the annual celebration in the spring of their exodus from Egypt, that saving and liberating event by which they had become a people. The fact that the death and resurrection of Jesus took place at Passover led Paul and others to interpret what had happened to Jesus as a new Passover, to see in it a new and definitive liberating act of God leading to a new covenant that would eventually embrace everyone who would accept it in faith.

In a number of European languages the words for Easter and Passover are the same. From an early date Easter, as the celebration of both the death and the resurrection of Jesus, became the center for Christians of their liturgical year. The special vigil ceremonies that marked it were regarded as a privileged moment for receiving new members into the community of faith through baptism.

If Easter was thus the first of the great Christian feasts, it was not long before people felt the need to set aside a special day to celebrate the birth of Jesus. The day chosen for this in eastern Christianity was January 6. The Latin or western church embraced the practice in the early fourth century and fixed its celebration on December 25. The choice of this date seems to have been related to pagan festivities in honor of the unconquerable sun and connected with the winter solstice. The Christian festival affirmed that Jesus was the true sun whose coming overcame the darkness of sin and death.

From the beginning Christmas celebrated more than the historical birth of Jesus. It was concerned with the mystery of his person. By this time Christian thought had come to focus on the fact of the incarnation, the taking on by the Word or Son of God of human form. His coming among us was understood to be in itself a saving event.

With Easter and Christmas in place, the church had what has turned out to be the basic frame for its liturgical year. Before long both feasts spilled over, as it were, into the weeks preceding and following them. Both were seen as so important as to require a period of preparation. Lent grew from a few days until it embraced the forty days that we now know. Its development was tied up with the immediate preparation of catechumens for baptism and with the growing sense that the whole community needed to prepare spiritually for the solemn celebration of the paschal mystery. The forty days recall both the forty years that Israel spent in the desert before entering the promised land and the forty days that Jesus prayed and fasted in the wilderness before beginning his public ministry.

Advent plays an analogous role in regard to Christmas. Its liturgy evokes both the hopes and the longings of Israel for a messiah and the age-old Christian conviction that someday Christ will return in glory. Like Lent, Advent has a certain penitential character in that it calls us to conversion of heart as we pray for the coming of Christ into our lives and into our world here and now.

The Easter celebration is extended over a period of seven weeks in what is known as the Easter season and which culminates with the feast of Pentecost. The coming of the Spirit marks the beginning of the time of the church. The period after Christmas is somewhat briefer but it too prolongs our celebration of the coming of Jesus and unfolds some of its implications. It includes special liturgies in honor of Mary the mother of God, the holy family, the epiphany, and the baptism of Jesus.

Those Sundays that belong to neither the Easter nor the Christmas cycles are known as Sundays in ordinary time. They are divided into two periods of unequal length falling between the end of the Christmas season and the beginning of Lent and between Pentecost and Advent.

The rhythm of the liturgical year continues even in our secular world to influence consciously and unconsciously our awareness and appropriation of the Christian mystery. An understanding and appreciation of its various moments and structure are crucial for a conscious and prayerful involvement in the Sunday eucharists.

The present book contains a series of reflections on the assigned biblical readings for the Sundays and major feasts of cycle A. They are in no sense technical although they have attempted to take advantage of the rich resource that contemporary biblical scholarship represents. They tend to stay fairly close to the texts without either presenting a simple paraphrase or going into any detailed exegesis. My desire has been to serve the biblical readings, not to offer an alternative to them. In most cases I have tried to draw out a theme or two and to show how it or they can give a certain unity to that particular day's liturgy.

My hope is that anyone wishing to deepen his or her involvement in the Sunday eucharist will find what I have written helpful. It should be of special interest to lectors preparing for their participation in the liturgy. The more their reading is informed by a genuine comprehension of the texts, the more effective it will be. Teachers and catechists who use the Sunday readings in class and group discussion should also find useful material here.

Vatican II insisted that the homily is an integral part of the eucharistic liturgy and that one should be given on all Sundays and major feasts. Good preaching does not come easily. It presupposes both a loving and a meditative involvement with the biblical texts and a sense of the congregation to whom one wants to communicate something of their meaning. The present reflections are not meant as homilies but they could well be of service to preachers in their preparation of them.

Much of what is contained in the present book first appeared in the form of a weekly column in the *Catholic Register*, a national Canadian publication produced in Toronto. I am grateful to the editor as well as to others who were involved in inviting me to write them. In addition to all the Sundays I have included sections on most of the major feasts. Those belonging to the Christmas and Easter cycles can be found in the chapters related to those feasts. The material on the Assumption of Mary, All Saints, and the Immaculate Conception appears in a separate section at the end. The readings listed at the beginning of each reflection correspond to those contained in the new edition of the lectionary published by the Canadian Bishops' Conference in 1992. This book completes a series of three volumes covering the entire three year cycle of Sunday readings.

Advent

He Comes

1ST SUNDAY OF ADVENT
Readings: Is 2:1-5, Rom 13:11-14, Mt 24:37-44

As a period of preparation for Christmas, Advent is a time of expectation and renewal. The very word "advent" suggests a coming or arrival. The texts for the next four Sundays refer both to the historical coming of Jesus in the past and to his return at the end of time. They also point to our need to be open to him as he comes into our lives here and now.

Today's gospel is taken from a longer discourse in which Jesus spoke about his future coming and about the final judgment that will accompany it. Our reading invites us to be alert and conscious and ready to welcome him when he comes. It draws a rather striking parallel between those who will experience the end time and those who were alive in the days of Noah. Then as now people tend to be caught up with everyday concerns and pleasures. Oblivious to what was happening around them, Noah's contemporaries were simply swept away when the floods fell upon them. So, too, in the future, Jesus says, will those who refuse to heed his warning be lost. Whether men or women, whether at work or play, some will be taken up into the kingdom while others will be left to their destruction.

The Armor of Light

Jesus encourages his hearers and us to be morally and spiritually awake as we await the time of his coming. What is required above all is a heightened sense of the ultimate meaning of life and a commitment to live in a way that corresponds to it. What concretely this involves is suggested by Jesus' account of the last judgment. There he makes clear that we will be judged according to how we have or have not responded to the needs of the poor, the hungry, the sick and the homeless.

Paul strikes very much the same note in the second reading. The time is growing short and the day of salvation is fast approaching. He begs us to lay aside the works of darkness, those things that undermine and destroy life, things like reckless pleasure and quarreling and jealousy. We must put on the armor of light, or, as he also phrases it, we must put on Jesus Christ. The verses immediately preceding our text make clear that the whole of the law can be summed up in the one great commandment of love of neighbor. Putting this into practice is the best possible preparation for the coming of Christ.

Wake from Sleep

The first generation of Christians had an acute sense of the nearness of the end. Many of them believed that the risen Jesus would soon return in power to establish God's kingdom. Although we continue to believe that human history is tending toward its final fulfillment in God, few of us expect that the end will come in our own lifetime. For us today's readings have a different meaning.

Jesus' warning about vigilance takes on special significance when we think about the moment of our death. In and through it we will encounter Christ and in doing so will undergo a judgment. How we will fare in that judgment will depend on how we live our lives now. To think about this should not be an occasion for sadness. It should simply remind us that in this world we have no lasting home. The realization that our destiny is to be with Christ for all eternity should motivate us here and now to imitate him and to live by his Spirit.

Walk in His Paths

In today's first reading Isaiah envisages a future time when Jerusalem will be widely recognized as God's special dwelling place and when peoples from distant lands will stream to it in order to learn how to walk in the ways of the Lord. These ways are marked above all by justice and peace. Weapons of war, he says, will be transformed into instruments of agriculture, into tools for feeding the hungry.

Our God, Advent proclaims, is a God who comes. He has come in the course of our individual and collective histories. He came in a unique and definitive way in Jesus. As the God of the future, he will continue to come into our life both now and at the end of time. If we really believe in such a God, then we ought to live with an awareness of him and of his comings.

All three of today's readings affirm our need to prepare for and to open ourselves to God's coming. Isaiah puts it simply: "Let us walk in the light of the Lord." For us, God's light has shone with unique intensity in the teaching and example of Jesus. There can be no better preparation for the coming of Christ than the effort to live according to his teaching.

Promise and Fulfillment

2ND SUNDAY OF ADVENT
Readings: Is 11:1-10, Rom 15:4-9, Mt 3:1-12

The person and ministry of John the Baptist embody much of what is involved in the Advent spirit. Like a prophet, he appears in the wilderness of Judea and calls people to conversion and renewal. Pointing beyond himself, he announces the coming of someone greater than he is, someone, as today's gospel puts it, who will baptize with the Holy Spirit and fire.

John is the forerunner, the one who prepares the way of the Lord. The gospels apply to him a text from the prophet Isaiah which, in speaking of the return of the people from exile, evokes the biblical experience of God as a God of salvation and liberation. There is a continuity between the exodus from Egypt, the return from exile in Babylon, and the coming of Jesus.

The God of the Bible is a God of promise. Abraham and Sarah are called to set out on a journey and are promised that in spite of their age their descendants will become a great people. God promises Moses that the Israelites will escape their slavery in Egypt and will inherit a rich and fertile land. Promise leads to fulfillment, and fulfillment becomes the basis for new promises.

A Shoot of Jesse

Today's reading from Isaiah is applied by Christians to the coming of Jesus. Although originally intended to point to some ideal king that would reign in the near future, it was recognized in time as embodying Israel's hope for the messiah, the anointed one, whose coming would usher in the definitive reign of God.

The prophet's dream is for justice and goodness, for just judgment against evildoers, and for mercy for the poor and the meek. The one to bring all this about will be endowed with a spirit of wisdom and understanding, of knowledge and fear of the Lord. His strength and passion for justice will be combined with compassion and utter fidelity to God's will and God's way.

The coming of such a king, the text affirms, will transform nature and create conditions that evoke paradise. A child will bring wild and domesticated animals together. The earth will be full of the glory and the knowledge of God. It is a dream of total and lasting peace, of wholeness and integrity, a vision of creation brought to fulfillment in God.

A Reason for Hope

Today's reading from Paul's letter to the Romans contains a word of hope and encouragement for the community to which it is addressed. Jewish and Gentile believers are urged to live in peace and harmony with one another. Their coming together in faith in Christ has been the work of God. It represents the fulfillment of the promises once made to the patriarchs and the prophets. Paul evokes the past in order to give hope for the future. The scriptures repeatedly bear witness to God's fidelity to his promises and in doing so assure us that the new promises of which we are the heirs will themselves one day be brought to fulfillment.

To say that God is a God of promise is to say that he is a God of history and of the future. He has a plan for us and for all of humankind and he will see that it is brought to completion. What happened in Israel's past became a basis for its hope in the future. What God did for us in Jesus Christ is a guarantee that God remains with us and that he is leading us to final fulfillment in him.

Expectation and Preparation

The liturgy of Advent is full of hope and longing. In its use of prophetic and other texts from the Old Testament, it tries to evoke a sense of waiting and watching, of desire and openness for Christ's coming. Although most of the texts speak of what took place in the past, their presence in the liturgy invites us to read them in terms of the present.

Christ comes here and now; he comes into our lives, into the world and into the community of the church. He comes in the word and the eucharist, in our mutual love and service, in our struggles for justice and peace, in our suffering and pain. He comes wherever people open themselves to the values preached by the prophets and embodied in his own life.

John the Baptist reminds us of the need to prepare for Christ's coming. He challenges the indifferent and the self-righteous among us and calls them and all of us to ever greater conversion. The coming of Christ always means both judgment and a new beginning. In order to welcome him into our world and to become instruments in the spread of his kingdom, we must learn to bear the fruit of love and justice in our lives.

Be Strong and Rejoice

3RD SUNDAY OF ADVENT
Readings: Is 35:1-6a, 10, Jas 5:7-10, Mt 11:2-11

In today's gospel, John the Baptist sends two messengers to ask Jesus whether or not he is "the one who is to come," the longed for messiah or Christ of Israel. Instead of answering directly, Jesus simply points to his teaching and activity. Tell John, he says, what you see and hear. For those with eyes to see, Jesus' life bears eloquent testimony to who he is.

The prophetic oracle that constitutes today's first reading is addressed to the people of the desert region south of Israel. It contains a promise of salvation. Be strong, Isaiah says; do not fear; your God is coming. His presence will bring fertility to the land and rejoicing and gladness to its people. The blind will see, the deaf will hear, the lame will walk and the mute will sing with joy.

The biblical God is a God of life and goodness and justice; his presence brings with it healing and wholeness and peace. Faith in such a God can strengthen those who are weak and make steadfast those who feel weighed down by the burdens of life. God's definitive coming will mean everlasting joy. "Sorrow and sighing shall flee away."

The Messiah's Deeds

Paraphrasing our first reading and one or two other passages of Isaiah, Jesus points to the miracles that he has worked and to his preaching of the good news among the poor as signs that with him the messianic times have indeed begun. He adds a rather enigmatic phrase: "Blessed is anyone who takes no offense at me."

The presence of Jesus demands a decision, a response, a choice between faith and unbelief. For some in his own day as well as in ours, Jesus is a stumbling block, a source of scandal,

someone in whom they are unable to recognize God's presence.
For others, it is very much the opposite. They believe that Jesus in
his life and teaching, in his love and fidelity, reveals and brings
among us the saving presence of God.

Contrary to expectations, the coming of the messiah did not
mean the end of human history and the definitive establishment
of God's reign. It did, however, mark a decisive stage in regard to
both. In Jesus God manifested his eternal love and acceptance of
us and planted among us a seed of new life, a seed that is meant
to bear fruit now and to be brought to fulfillment in eternity.

Be Patient

Today's second reading reveals some of the tensions that
faith in Jesus as the messiah created among the first Christians.
They thought that he would soon return and usher in God's
kingdom in all its glory. When he did not, and when their own
struggles and pains continued, they tended to grow weary and
to lose some of their joy and enthusiasm.

James counsels patience. Like the farmer waiting for the fall
and spring rain, believers need to be patient about the coming of
the Lord. He will surely come. What is important is that in the
interim people live in ways that correspond to and reflect his
gifts. They should neither quarrel nor grumble but take as an
example of patience the prophets, so many of whom suffered in
the course of fulfilling their ministry.

A Messianic People

John the Baptist is both a prophet and someone in whom
the prophetic vocation has been brought to its fulfillment. He her-
alds the coming of the messiah. With Jesus and above all with his
death and resurrection and with the outpouring of the divine
Spirit, God establishes a new covenant with us. In doing so he
brings into existence the church as a community rooted in and
called to live out of the new life made available in Christ.

Faith in Jesus involves a certain tension between what has
already been given and its fulfillment at the end of time in God. It

is a tension that applies both to us as individuals and to the church as a whole. Renewed by what has been given us in Christ we remain subject to the burdens of time and history.

Advent reminds us of the historical coming of Jesus and of all that it has meant and means to us. It also points ahead to his future coming and to our final fulfillment in God. Living as we do between these two moments, we are to be witnesses in all that we are and do to Christ's gifts. Individually and as a church we are called to be people of faith and love and service. To the degree that we are, we become signs and sacraments of Christ's healing and renewing presence among us. Rooted in faith, our patience in the face of difficulties is not passive but active. It is a source of strength and of courage.

Who Is Jesus?

4TH SUNDAY OF ADVENT
Readings: Is 7:10-14, Rom 1:1-7, Mt 1:18-24

The liturgy for the last Sunday of Advent invites us to reflect in a special way on the person and identity of the one whose birth we are to celebrate at Christmas. The gospel highlights the person of Joseph and his perplexity in discovering that Mary is pregnant. A revelation from God reassures him and reveals the deep meaning of the miracle that is unfolding.

Joseph is addressed by the angel as "son of David." It is through Joseph's connection with the ancient royal family of Israel that Jesus will be known by the same title. For Jews, legal parentage had rights very much like those of natural parentage. The child to be born will be Joseph's legal son, but, the text insists, he will be God's Son as well.

Joseph is told that it is by the power of the Spirit that Jesus has been conceived. Mary's virginity expresses in a concrete and forceful way that Jesus will be both our brother according to the flesh and in a unique way the child of God. For this reason Joseph is to give the child the name Jesus, a name suggestive of his future saving role.

God with Us

In a way that is typical of him, Matthew concludes his account of the incident and reinforces its meaning by quoting a passage from the prophet Isaiah. It is a text that is contained in today's first reading. Originally proclaimed in the eighth century B.C. to a godless king as a promise and sign of God's continuing presence with the people, Matthew sees in it a foretelling of the birth of the messiah.

For Matthew the somewhat vague reference in the original passage to a young woman has become a prophecy of Mary's virginal conception. The child that will be born of her will be called Emmanuel. In him God will be truly with us.

Although Christian art and piety have tended to focus almost exclusively on the mother and child, Matthew stresses the role of Joseph. As little as we know of him, he remains a remarkable figure. He is, the text says, a just or righteous man, a good man intent on doing what is right by his young wife. He tries to the best of his ability to respond to and to cooperate with the mysterious ways of God as these become known to him.

The Gospel of God

The message of today's second reading is very similar to that of the gospel. In his letter to the Romans, Paul is writing to a community which he had not founded but which he hopes to visit. The opening verses of the letter present him and his mission. He describes himself as a servant or slave of Christ, as an apostle set apart to proclaim the gospel of God.

The good news that Paul preaches is focused entirely on the person and destiny of Jesus. He is the Son of God descended from David according to the flesh and manifested as the divine Son with power from the moment of his resurrection from the dead. For Paul the resurrection represents a decisive turning point in the life and mission of Jesus. Having entered into God's glory, Jesus is able to share with us his holiness and life.

Paul associates the resurrection of Jesus with the work of the Spirit. As with the birth of Jesus, so too with the resurrection, the Spirit has an active role to play. It is the Spirit that binds together the human son of David with the divine Son and who makes the risen Christ the source of new life for us.

Grace and Peace

In spite of all the other things that Christmas means in our culture, what it finally celebrates is the birth and person of Jesus Christ. In Jesus God entered into and became one with a human life like our own. In doing so he drew near to each and every one of us. He gave us a new dignity and revealed to us our ultimate destiny. We are called in Christ to be God's children.

The first of the great Christian feasts to be celebrated was Easter. It recalled both the death and resurrection of Jesus and the salvation and reconciliation that they entailed. It was only in the experience of the new life in the Spirit that became ours through the paschal mystery that Christians began to understand the depths of the mystery of Jesus' person.

Christmas presupposes the experience of Easter. Matthew's gospel builds on and gives deeper meaning to the creed proclaimed by Paul. From his birth Jesus is both son of David and Son of God. The coming of Jesus then and now, his coming in the flesh and his coming into our hearts, can only mean grace and peace for those who open themselves to him in faith and in love.

The Christmas Season

A Child Is Born

CHRISTMAS —
MASS DURING THE NIGHT
Readings: Is 9:2-4, 6-7, Tit 2:11-14, Lk 2:1-16

The Christmas liturgy is quite distinctive in the extent to which a sense of radiant joy permeates it. It runs through all three of the Christmas masses and spills over into the carols and visual imagery that we associate in our different traditions with this time of the year. At the heart of it all is something that is both ordinary and extraordinary. A young woman gives birth to her first child. If such an event is most often an occasion of joy for those involved in it, the celebration of the birth of Jesus is for Christians particularly joyful because of what he and his life mean for us and for all of humankind.

Luke's account of what took place is brief and straightforward. Mary gave birth to her first-born son and wrapped him in bands of cloth and laid him in a manger. The context within which the event is situated hints at its significance. The references to the emperor Augustus and to the governor of Syria suggest that although Jesus was born in a distant corner of the empire, his life will have implications that are worldwide. The presence of Mary and Joseph in Bethlehem underlines that Jesus is of the house of David. He is related to the line of the kings of Israel from which God's messiah is to come.

The Angelic Message

The fact and the significance of Jesus' birth are announced first of all not to civil or religious leaders but to shepherds caring for their flocks in neighboring fields. Although there is no indication that they are particularly poor, it is clear that they stand for simple, average people. The source of their knowledge is not their

23

own insight or understanding but God's revelation. An angel of the Lord appears to them and proclaims "good news of great joy for all the people."

In revealing the identity of the child the angel uses three terms that will be central to the explicitly Christian faith that develops after the resurrection. Jesus is the Christ or messiah, the anointed one of God who fulfills the hopes of Israel and who will bring about God's kingdom. More than that, he is the Lord, someone who shares in a special way in the dignity and rule of God himself. The reason for his coming is summed up in the third title: He is the Savior of humankind.

A Light Has Shone

Today's first reading also celebrates the birth of a child. Writing near the end of the eighth century B.C., Isaiah sees in the newborn successor to the king of Judah a promise of hope against the oppression of the power of Assyria. The language is wonderfully poetic. Darkness will give way to light and a suffering people will rejoice the way farm workers do at harvest time.

The child will become a great and just king who will be for his people like a strong and caring father. The fruit of his life will be enduring peace. All this will come about because of God's presence with him.

As so often happens, Isaiah came with time to recognize that his hopes and dreams were beyond what the new king would ever be able to achieve. More and more this text and others were read as referring to a future offspring of David who would be God's effective instrument in bringing about lasting peace. It is not difficult to see why Christians came to see in the text a veiled promise of Jesus and his saving work.

The Revelation of God's Grace

The reading from the letter to Titus reminds us that our celebration is not just of a past event. If we remember the birth of Jesus it is first of all because of what we believe his whole life meant and means for us. He is the revelation of God's grace, the

one through whom God has granted us forgiveness and reconciliation and called us "to become a people of his own, zealous for
good deeds."

Central therefore to our celebration of Christmas is a recognition of the new life that the coming of Jesus has made possible
for us. Paul describes Jesus as the first-born of many sisters and
brothers. Through his death and resurrection he has become a
living Spirit present and active among us, calling us to share his
life in faith and love.

The Christmas liturgy invites us to open our minds and
hearts to the risen Christ so that he may continue to be born in us.
To be a Christian is to put on Christ, to be animated by his Spirit.
For people of faith, the coming of Jesus marks the beginning of a
new humanity, a new creation. May our celebration of his birth
renew his life in us, our families, and our world.

Peace and Love

FEAST OF THE HOLY FAMILY
Readings: Sir 3:2-6, 12-14, Col 3:12-21, Mt 2:13-15, 19-23

Today's feast celebrates and invites us to reflect on the human and religious bonds that grounded the life together of Mary, Joseph and Jesus. In doing so it reminds us of the various families to which we belong: the human family, the family of the church, and our own immediate and extended families.

The gospel reading this year focuses on Joseph and on the role he played in protecting and caring for the child Jesus. For Matthew, the themes of conflict and rejection that were to be so much a part of Jesus' public life were present even at his birth. Herod is threatened at the news that a child destined to be king has been born and he seeks to destroy him.

Joseph, like his namesake in the time of the patriarchs, is an interpreter of dreams. Discerning God's will in them, he acts immediately. The fate of his family has been the fate of untold families throughout history. They are obliged to become refugees and to flee in order to escape violence and destruction. In some strange way Jesus is meant to relive the destinies of Israel and of Moses. Like the people of old he is called out of Egypt and like Moses he escapes the hand of a cruel pharaoh.

Forgiveness and Love

Most of today's second reading is addressed to the Christian community as a whole. It suggests the kind of relations that ideally, given our common faith and our common life in Christ, should exist among us. The text does not begin by telling us how to act but rather by reminding us what and who we are.

We have been chosen and loved by God and we have been

made holy in the depths of our being by the presence of God's Spirit in us. Because this is so, we must try to live in a way that corresponds to it. We ought to treat one another with compassion and kindness, with forbearance and patience. As standardized as such a list of virtues might seem, it is by no means arbitrary.

The Christian community is not to be marked by backbiting or self-righteousness but by mutual acceptance and forgiveness. The text echoes the Our Father in recommending that we forgive others as the Lord has forgiven us. Above all, it says, we must clothe ourselves with love. This, again, is not an empty phrase. It expresses the heart of the teaching of Jesus.

Being a Family

The reality of most of our families is very far from such an ideal. Many of us are broken and wounded people, and what we bring therefore to family life is anything but perfect. Many families are marked by division and tension. It might be due to divorce or separation or the death of a spouse. It might be because a family member is involved in drugs or some other self-destructive pattern of behavior.

The gospel ideal is less about any particular form of family life and more about the way that we can and ought to live whatever the concrete situation in which we find ourselves. The Christian understanding of life presupposes a sense of sin, an awareness of the power of evil at work in the world, undermining our best efforts to do what is good.

Christ comes as a healer and reconciler. He brings forgiveness and the possibility of a new beginning. He reveals that God loves us and that we are called to a new and better life. His challenge is not an easy one, but it is possible because of the gift of the Spirit that he offers us.

The Family of the Church

Vatican II speaks of the family as the domestic church. It is in the family that we are called first of all and in a special way to live the values that Jesus preached. The family, on the other hand, is a model of what our life as church could be. In the third eucharistic prayer we ask God to hear the prayers of the family gathered before him and to unite all his children wherever they may be.

To believe in God and to believe in ourselves as made in God's image and likeness is to have every reason to think of all people as our sisters and brothers. We all belong to a single family, to God's family. The coming of Jesus means for us the coming of God, the coming of the renewing, healing, and transforming love of God among us.

In Christ and through the gift of his Spirit we share in God's nature and become in a more intimate way God's children. The unity that is ours at the level of Christ's Spirit should overflow into our actual, everyday relations with one another. When it does, these will be marked by forgiveness and love.

Pondering in Her Heart

JANUARY 1 — MARY, MOTHER OF GOD
Readings: Num 6:22-27, Gal 4:4-7, Lk 2:16-21

The liturgical year begins not with January 1 but with the first Sunday of Advent. This is why, to a large degree, today's liturgy disregards the theme of the new year. Its focus continues to be still very much on Christmas. According to an ancient Jewish as well as Christian practice, celebrations of major feasts or festivals last eight days. Their octave is always marked with special solemnity.

Today's gospel picks up more or less where that of the first mass at Christmas left off. It tells of the coming of the shepherds to Bethlehem and of their reaction to what they find there. It ends with a reference to the circumcision and naming of Jesus on the eighth day after his birth. It emphasizes that the name of Jesus comes not from his parents but from God. It was the name given by the angel before he was conceived.

As the mother of the child whose birth we celebrate, Mary is a central figure throughout the Christmas season. Today's liturgy draws our attention to the profound mystery involved in her maternity. It proclaims her as the mother of God. This is a title which, while not found as such in the scriptures, reflects Christian faith about the ultimate identity of Jesus.

Born of a Woman

Today's second reading, taken from the letter to the Galatians, is part of a much larger argument about justification coming not through the law but through grace. Paul reminds us that the coming of Jesus marked a new moment in God's plan of salvation. From now on it is through faith in Christ and baptism in his name that we are to receive the gift of the Spirit.

Although Jesus is the Son of God, he was born of a woman and born under the law. What Paul wants to emphasize here is that Jesus shared our humanity and more specifically that he came as a Jew subject to the law of Moses. In doing so, he offered salvation to those who lived under the law.

One way of expressing the gift that Jesus brought is to say that we who believe in him are empowered to become his sisters and brothers. This becomes possible through the gift of the Spirit. By sharing his Spirit we are able to enter into the intimacy of his relationship with God and to become with him children of God and heirs of eternal life.

Mary Treasured These Words

The statement that Jesus was born of a woman is the only reference in all of Paul's writings to Mary. She and her role loom much larger in Luke's account of Jesus' birth and childhood. There she is invited by God to become the mother of the Savior. Her believing and willing acceptance of God's invitation is an essential moment in the unfolding of salvation.

Today's gospel uses a phrase that will return in the account of the finding of the boy Jesus in the temple. There it is said that Mary "treasured all these things in her heart." Her conscious and loving involvement in what is happening reflects a lively faith and a deep personal commitment.

If Mary is the mother of the Word incarnate and therefore the mother of God, she remains very much someone like ourselves, someone called to live by faith and not by vision. In many ways she is a model of what it is to be a believer. She cherishes her religious experience and ponders its meaning. It is only thus that believers can come to discern more precisely what God is doing in their lives and how they are to respond to it.

The Lord Bless You

Today's first reading contains in the words of a blessing one of the most beautiful of biblical prayers. Moses is directed by God to instruct the priestly family of Aaron how they are to bless the

Israelites. They are to ask God to look kindly on them, be present to them and give them the gift of shalom or peace. The word "peace" here means much more than the simple absence of war. It suggests the fullness of life. One might translate it as wholeness or well being. It more or less implies all that we mean by justice, peace, and love.

What the priests of Israel are privileged to do for their people is something that we all as members of Christ's priestly body might well do for one another. To bless a child or a spouse or a friend is to pray to God for his or her well-being. It is to ask God to pour out his blessings on them. This could and should be the deep meaning of our new year's greetings to one another. As believers we know how much we depend on God. May our greetings and good wishes be in fact prayers and blessings.

A Divine Presence

EPIPHANY OF THE LORD
Readings: Is 60:1-6, Eph 3:2-3a, 5-6, Mt 2:1-12

Unlike Luke, Matthew tells us almost nothing about the actual birth of Jesus. He is much more interested, as the account of the magi in today's gospel makes clear, in suggesting the impact that Jesus' life would eventually have. Rejected by the likes of Herod, Jesus will one day be recognized by the Gentiles as God's saving gift to the whole of humankind.

Although intimately connected in the liturgy to the story of the magi, the word "epiphany" in itself has a much broader meaning. It suggests an appearance or manifestation. When applied to God it points to something very similar to what we mean when we speak of God's self-revelation. The New Testament uses it to describe the second coming of Christ.

In recalling the birth of Jesus, what we are celebrating ultimately is the deepest mystery of his person. He was, as the letter to the Hebrews puts it, a human being like us in all things but sin. He was, in other words, our brother. And yet he was more than that. In Jesus the Word or Son of God entered into and embraced a human life and in doing so gave God a human face.

A Mystery of Reconciliation

In today's second reading Paul speaks of a mystery, hidden from all eternity in God, but now made manifest in Christ. This mystery is God's plan of salvation, God's purpose in creating. To believe in God at all is to believe that behind the sound and fury, the chaos and violence of life, there is a divine purpose working itself out.

The mystery as revealed in Christ is a mystery of forgiveness and reconciliation. Human beings are made for love and union with God and with one another. Christ came to destroy sin and to draw together all things and all people in himself. He has torn down the dividing wall of hostility that separates us from one another and made it possible for us to become one with him, to form with him a single body.

In keeping with today's gospel our passage from Ephesians emphasizes the fact that in Christ Gentiles as well as Jews are called to be heirs of God's kingdom. The traditional enmity that existed between these groups stands for all human division. In Christ our destiny, no matter what our race, sex, color or social status, is to be brothers and sisters of one another.

The Glory of the Lord

Today's first reading, from the third part of Isaiah, is full of hope and promise of a future manifestation of God in Jerusalem. The glory and the beauty of God will transform the city and make it and its inhabitants radiant and full of joy. God's coming, like a fresh and bright dawn, will banish darkness and bathe everything in its light.

The city itself will be an epiphany and will attract people from near and far. Jews and Gentiles will come streaming to it in order to worship the God whose presence has so transformed it. For Matthew the dream of the prophet about Jerusalem has become a reality in the person of Jesus.

John's gospel, more than any of the others, speaks of Jesus in terms of glory. The whole purpose of his life is to give glory to the Father; as he does so, the Father will glorify him. The glory that will be evident at his death and resurrection is a glory that belongs to him as the Word incarnate. To see his glory is to see the glory of the Father's only Son.

Revealed Yet Hidden

The story of the magi is bathed in a mysterious radiance, the radiance of the star, but even more importantly the radiance of God's presence in human form, the radiance of Jesus as the manifestation of God's saving will for us. This, however, is not all there is to the story. It begins and ends with a reference to King Herod.

The coming of the magi is inseparable from the violence of Herod and from the flight of Jesus and his parents to escape it. The epiphany of God in Jesus was more hidden and mysterious than one might have expected. The light that shone in it was not so overwhelming as to dispel all darkness.

The feast of Epiphany invites us to renew our faith in the appearing of God in the life of Jesus Christ. It reminds us that individually and as the church we are called to share in and continue what he began. We are to be signs and sacraments of what he brought into human life. The radiance of our churches at Christmastime should find an echo and an extension in the radiance of the goodness and kindness of our lives.

The Word Made Flesh

2ND SUNDAY AFTER CHRISTMAS
Readings: Sir 24:1-4, 8-12, Eph 1:3-6, 15-19, Jn 1:1-18

In contrast with Mark who begins his gospel with the preaching of John the Baptist and an account of the baptism of Jesus, Matthew and Luke begin with two chapters dealing with the conception and birth of the messiah. In spite of all their differences, both emphasize ways in which Jesus fulfills the hopes and expectations of Israel and suggest something of the uniqueness of his person. He is Christ and Savior, Son and Lord.

In the famous prologue that begins John's gospel and that constitutes today's third reading, the mystery of Jesus is sought behind his birth in the very life of God. The experience of the resurrection gave the first Christians a new lens for understanding Jesus and his mission. Everything that he had said and done while he was alive convinced them that he had come from God and that he spoke the word and wisdom of God. The fact that God had raised him up and made him manifest as Christ and Lord helped them gradually to realize that what he had become he already was from the moment of his birth. They knew that in Jesus they had encountered something more than a prophet or holy man. In him God's wisdom and Word had taken on human flesh.

Lady Wisdom

The book of Sirach from which today's first reading is taken belongs to a group of biblical writings known as wisdom literature. Much of what they contain is made up of commonsense reflections on how one might live a good life. Occasionally, however, they become more poetic and theological and describe and celebrate divine wisdom portrayed as a female figure.

In these books wisdom is presented as someone who was

35

created by God before everything else. She rejoiced and played in God's presence. Through her God created the world and then sent her to dwell in the midst of it. She entered into the souls of the just and made them friends of God.

In our text wisdom is said to have come forth from the mouth of God. Although present to all things, God wanted her to dwell in a special way with the people of Israel. She set up her tent in Jerusalem and gave form and direction to the worship of the temple. She inspired the Torah or law that was meant to guide the life both of individuals and of the people.

Grace and Truth

The theme of the word of God is well known throughout the Bible. In the creation account in the first chapter of Genesis we are told that God spoke and that everything came to be. The prophets proclaimed God's word as something powerful and active. It consoles and challenges and brings about what it announces.

In his prologue John goes beyond the kind of personification of God's wisdom and word that can be found in the Jewish tradition. For him the Word can be both identified with God and distinguished from God. Elsewhere he uses the analogy of Father and Son to suggest the relationship between the Word and God.

For John, the Word of God was and is active in creation and human history and in a special way in the life of Israel. In Jesus that same Word has become flesh, taken on human form, embraced and experienced a life like ours. Jesus is truly human and yet uniquely one with God. He both reveals God and communicates to those who believe in him a share in God's life.

Chosen in Christ

Today's second reading is an excerpt from a longer prayer of praise and thanksgiving that begins the letter to the Ephesians. It has obvious parallels with John's prologue except that now the focus is less on the Word and his activity than on the relationship that God has established from all eternity in Christ with us. Paul describes the God whom he blesses as the Father of our Lord

Jesus Christ. He has chosen us in Christ and destined us to be his adopted children.

Christmas in our culture is many things. For believers it celebrates the birth of Jesus, the Son and Word of God in human form. The incarnation recapitulates in some way the whole of God's creative and saving activity. The Word through whom all things were made is the divine reality through which humanity is to be healed and brought home to God. If we were chosen by God before the foundation of the world, it was so that we might share his life both in this world and in eternity.

Our text ends with a prayer that God will give us wisdom and understanding in order that we might know the gift that is ours now and the glorious inheritance that still awaits us. This is a prayer that we might well make for one another.

The Beloved Son

BAPTISM OF THE LORD
Readings: Is 42:1-4, 6-7, Acts 10:34-38, Mt 3:13-17

Although the first Christians all remembered the baptism of Jesus by John as the beginning of Jesus' public ministry, some wondered why the messiah should have submitted to a baptism that had been preached for the repentance of sin. In his account of the event, Matthew tries to respond to their concern by having John protest that it is he who should be baptized by Jesus rather than Jesus by him.

The meaning of Jesus' response to John is not immediately clear: he is willing to be baptized in order "to fulfill all righteousness." The phrase probably points to a desire on Jesus' part to recognize the providential role of John and the continuing significance of the conversion to which he calls people. For the evangelists what is most important about Jesus' baptism is the theophany or divine manifestation that accompanies it.

The opening of the heavens indicates that a new moment in God's relation to humankind is beginning. The coming of the Spirit in the form of a dove is reminiscent of the first verses of Genesis where it is said that a wind or God's Spirit hovered over the waters. With Jesus a new creation is about to begin.

The Servant of God

The highpoint of the event is the proclamation by the voice from heaven: "This is my Son, the Beloved, with whom I am well pleased." The phrase is rich in biblical references. The word "beloved" was used to describe Isaac, the son Abraham was asked to sacrifice, while the language of sonship occurs in the psalms and elsewhere with reference to a kingly heir of David.

Today's liturgy emphasizes a third reference, this one to the servant of God evoked in a number of poems in the latter part of the book of Isaiah. The first of these constitutes today's first reading. Its presence in the liturgy suggests that it has something to say to us about Jesus' life and mission.

In Isaiah the servant is sometimes the people of Israel and sometimes an individual. In our reading the Lord announces that he delights in his servant and that he will send his Spirit upon him. The servant has a mission. It is to bring justice to the world, to be an instrument of God's saving activity, to be for all peoples a light and a revelation of God's will.

Anointed with the Spirit

The reference to the Spirit in all three readings invites us to reflect on the Spirit's role in the ministry of Jesus. The second reading contains the first part of a sermon of Peter in which he for the first time proclaims the gospel to a Gentile family. He says that, although God sent his message of peace first to Israel, it is meant for all peoples.

The ministry of Jesus began when he was anointed with the Holy Spirit. Because of the Spirit's presence with him, Jesus went about doing good and healing those oppressed by the devil. If Jesus is God's servant, sent to proclaim God's saving justice, he accomplishes his ministry through the power of God's Spirit.

Although Jesus is the Word incarnate, truly God and truly human, his coming among us is inseparable from the work of the Spirit. While the creed affirms that he was conceived by the power of the Holy Spirit, today's readings insist that his life and ministry were what they were because of the continuing presence of the Spirit to him.

The Trinity and Salvation

Although it would be an anachronism to see behind Matthew's account of the baptism a fully developed doctrine of the Trinity, it is not hard to understand why Christians through the centuries have recognized in it a revelation of the trinitarian nature of God. The reference to the Son implies a Father. The Spirit is the bond that unites them.

The trinitarian dimension of God's involvement with us in Christ is also affirmed in the second reading. Salvation begins with God. It is God who sent Jesus and who anointed him with the Holy Spirit. In the light of the whole of Jesus' life and mission and especially of his death and resurrection, he was recognized by the apostles and the first believers as "Lord of all." As human as he was, he belongs to the world of God.

Salvation comes from God in Jesus Christ and through the power of God's Spirit. Recognition of this led Christians to realize that the only adequate way for them to profess faith in God was to confess him as a mystery of Father, Son and Spirit. In that threefold name we are baptized and in being baptized are associated with the saving reality of the baptism of Jesus.

Ordinary Time:
Sundays 2 to 8

Sent by God

2ND SUNDAY IN ORDINARY TIME
Readings: Is 49:3, 5-6, 1 Cor 1:1-3, Jn 1:29-34

In the preface to John's gospel, John the Baptist is described as a man sent by God to give testimony to the light. The bulk of his testimony is contained in today's gospel reading. John points to Jesus as the Lamb of God who takes away the sins of the world. As well known as the phrase is from the liturgy of the eucharist, its precise meaning in our text is unclear.

Some scholars refer it to the lamb that was a part of the Passover meal and that recalled the lamb whose blood was used in the events of the exodus to keep the angel of death from the houses of the people. Others relate it to what Isaiah says in chapter 52 about the servant of God who is rejected and suffers and dies because of our sins. Like a lamb he is led to the slaughter. The book of Revelation refers to the risen Christ as the lamb once slain but who dies no more.

In some sense all of these themes are evoked by John's witness. Jesus will be a victim but a victim who will triumph. His death will bring about a new exodus and a new covenant. He is the true servant of God who will suffer for our transgressions and win for us God's forgiveness.

The Spirit Remains

John the Baptist testifies that he saw the Spirit descend upon Jesus. He emphasizes, moreover, that the coming of the Spirit was no passing phenomenon. It remained with Jesus, and because it did Jesus will be able, once he has passed through the crucible of his death and resurrection, to pour out the same Spirit on us. He will baptize not simply with water as John did, but with the Holy Spirit.

The passage ends with the affirmation that Jesus is the Son of God or, as some texts put it, God's chosen one. In either case Jesus is called and sent by God. He comes to reveal the mystery of God and to bring forgiveness and new life.

Today's first reading underlines the theme of the servant. Formed by God in his mother's womb, the servant is sent to gather the scattered tribes of Israel and to be "a light to the nations." Through him God's salvation will reach to the ends of the earth. All of this has become a reality in Jesus.

Called To Be Saints

Over the next several weeks our second reading will be taken from Paul's first letter to the Corinthians. Today's text contains its opening verses. Although its language might seem to us self-evident and almost a platitude, it points to distinctive features of the Christian experience of salvation in Christ.

Like the prophets and John the Baptist, Paul sees himself as someone who is called by God, in his case, called to be an apostle. Apostle in Greek means literally someone who is sent. Paul has been sent to preach the good news of Christ and to gather believers into the church of God. The Greek word for church suggests a coming together of people in response to a call.

Paul describes the community at Corinth as made up of people who have been sanctified, people who have been made holy in Christ. Through faith and baptism they have received Christ's Spirit and have become members of Christ's body. At the same time they are called to grow in holiness, to become saints, to live as disciples of Jesus. To help them as they struggle to do so, Paul prays that they will be filled with grace and peace.

The Living God

All three readings presuppose and express a certain experience of God. The God of Israel and the Father of Jesus Christ is in no sense distant or indifferent. He is a living God, a God of freedom and love, a God intensely concerned about humankind. He calls people to be servants and instruments of his saving activity.

John the Baptist is in many ways like the great prophets of old. Chosen in his mother's womb, he is sent to proclaim God's will and to call people to faith and conversion. What makes his mission distinctive is the immediate testimony that he gives to Jesus as the messiah. Jesus, more than anyone, is the recipient of a divine call and mission. His whole life reflects the nearness of God and God's concern for us.

Paul's sense of God is like that of the prophets and of the Baptist and to some degree of Jesus. He too is called and given a mission. What is true of Paul is true in different ways of all believers. Endowed with Christ's Spirit we are called to live in such a way as to bear witness to God's love for us and to the salvation that has become ours in Jesus Christ.

The Good News

3RD SUNDAY IN ORDINARY TIME
Readings: Is 9:1-4, 1 Cor 1:10-13, 17-18, Mt 4:12-23

Today's gospel contains Matthew's account of the beginning of the public ministry of Jesus. After his baptism by John and the forty days in the desert, he returns to Galilee and more specifically to Capernaum, a town on the northwest shore of the Sea of Galilee. In beginning his preaching there, he fulfills a prophecy of Isaiah, the text of which is quoted in the gospel and at somewhat greater length in the first reading.

An extended version of the passage from Isaiah is part of the liturgy for the first mass at Christmas. The coming of God, it affirms, means light and joy for all who welcome it. Darkness will be overcome, sadness banished and the weight of oppression lifted from the shoulders of those suffering under it. All this begins to be fulfilled in the preaching of Jesus.

Matthew tells us that Jesus went throughout Galilee teaching in synagogues, proclaiming the gospel or good news of the kingdom and curing those who were sick. The heart and center of his mission and ministry are summed up in the words: "Repent, for the kingdom of heaven is at hand."

The Kingdom of Heaven

Where the other evangelists prefer the phrase "the kingdom of God," Matthew speaks of "the kingdom of heaven." The change reflects his Jewish heritage with its profound reverence for the name of God. A word like "heaven" evokes God without actually naming him. The meaning, however, of the two phrases is the same.

Jesus announces that the kingdom or reign of God is at hand, has come near, is on the point of breaking in. The image is rooted in biblical history. God is like a king, and his coming will entail the establishment of his reign. The presence of the kingdom will mean peace and forgiveness and a renewal of life. The cures that Jesus works are signs that in him God's healing power is active in the world.

The first word that Jesus preaches is repent, be converted. Mark spells out a little more fully the response that Jesus wants with the phrase, "Repent and believe in the good news." Whatever the formulation, the coming of God's kingdom demands something of us. We must turn and open ourselves to it, welcome it into our lives and live in a way that corresponds to God's will.

The Cross of Christ

As today's second reading indicates, Jesus' preaching of the nearness of God's kingdom is replaced in Paul by an emphasis on the cross of Christ. It is through the death and resurrection of Jesus that salvation has been effected. God's forgiving and healing power come to us in a special way through the cross.

In our text Paul begs the members of the Christian community at Corinth to lead a life worthy of the calling to which they have been called. Made one in Christ, they ought to live in peace and union with one another. Tragically, however, they are divided. Groups and cliques have formed, the members of which identify with one or other of their preachers.

Paul repudiates any effort of his converts to use him in such a way. He is not the Savior. He was sent to preach not himself but Christ and Christ crucified. What some perceive as the foolishness of his message is in fact the wisdom of God. People of faith recognize in the cross God's saving power.

Fishers of People

Matthew includes in his account of the beginning of the preaching of Jesus the story of the call of the first disciples. The scene is a familiar one. Jesus sees Peter and Andrew casting their nets into the lake and invites them to follow him; they do. James and John receive the same invitation and immediately leave their boat and father in order to be with Jesus.

Matthew gives no indication whether the two sets of brothers had ever heard Jesus speak. His interest is not biographical but theological. People do not choose to follow Jesus out of self-interest or curiosity. He calls them. Jesus radiates such authority that when it erupts into a person's life, everything for that person is irrevocably changed.

Both sets of brothers followed Jesus in the most literal of ways. As true disciples they left everything in order to be with him and to learn from him and to share his life. From the beginning Jesus makes clear that their discipleship will involve them actively in his mission. They will become fishers of people. It is a vocation to which Paul and untold numbers after him in the course of church history have been called. Discipleship and some form of missionary activity are inseparable.

The Beatitudes

4TH SUNDAY IN ORDINARY TIME
Readings: Zeph 2:3; 3:12-13, 1 Cor 1:26-31, Mt 5:1-12a

Matthew's account of the sermon on the mount is probably the best known of the many collections of the teachings of Jesus in the New Testament. Situated near the beginning of his public life, it sets the tone for all that is to follow. The fact that it takes place on a mountain gives it an added solemnity. It was after all on Mount Sinai that the commandments were given to Moses and that the covenant was sealed.

The sermon begins with the beatitudes. Various groups of people, or rather people sharing certain attitudes or involved in certain activities, are declared by Jesus to be happy or blessed. They are blessed by God now and will be blessed even more in the future at the time of the definitive coming of God's kingdom.

With both their form and their content rooted in biblical history, the beatitudes introduce and exemplify a major theme of the whole sermon, namely that Jesus has come not to destroy but to fulfill the law and the prophets. He reaffirms what is deepest in Jewish piety and in the Jewish sense of God and declares that in spite of the sufferings and apparent abandonment of the little ones of this world, God continues to care for them.

The Remnant of Israel

Today's first reading contains striking parallels with the beatitudes. In his prophecy Zephaniah warns the powerful and the unjust that the coming day of the Lord will be for them a day of judgment and wrath. For those, however, whom he describes as the humble and the lowly, it will mean salvation.

The basic religious attitude that the prophet encourages could be called poverty of spirit. The proud and the self-righteous, those who subtly and not so subtly think of themselves almost as gods, feel no need for the living God and refuse to walk in his ways. Those on the other hand who know their vulnerability and limitations turn to God for help and strength.

If humility is at the root of an authentic religious attitude, it must also bear fruit in obedience to God's commandments. The prophet insists on the importance of speaking the truth and of doing what is just. Those who do this constitute a holy remnant, a small but vibrant group of true friends of God. Their presence hallows the whole people.

Humility and Justice

In the first beatitude Matthew speaks of the "poor in spirit" where Luke refers simply to the poor. The poverty on which Matthew insists is more than economic. It will often presuppose such poverty but it includes a spiritual element as well, a sense of humility, an awareness of one's utter nakedness before the holiness of God.

Matthew transforms Luke's beatitude about hunger into a statement about those who hunger and thirst for righteousness or justice. Such people suffer under and mourn violence and injustice and long for a manifestation of God's righteousness and for the establishment of true justice and peace among people.

Those who truly care for their neighbors and for God's world are usually also meek and merciful. Morality, moreover, for them is not simply external but rather permeates and purifies the heart. At the time of Jesus as today, people with such attitudes do not tend to achieve much success according to the standards of the world. And yet Jesus calls them blessed.

Boast in the Lord

Today's second reading suggests that what was true when Jesus began his preaching remained true in the experience of early Christianity. It was not the rich and the powerful but rather the weak and the simple who ordinarily accepted the message about salvation from God in Jesus Christ. Paul rejoices that this is in fact the case because it underlines our total dependence on God.

For Paul, salvation and meaning are to be found not in our own efforts and struggles but in God's gift. It is God, he says, who is the source of our life in Christ Jesus. God sent Christ to us as our wisdom and our redemption. The goodness and holiness of life to which we are called are possible only in Christ. Any boasting that we do must be done "in the Lord."

It would be a total misunderstanding of Jesus and Paul if in some perverted way one were to take pride in one's humility. True humility demands self-forgetfulness. Real concern for others, genuine openness to life in all its dimensions, absolute honesty about one's vulnerability: such things bring poverty of spirit and an awareness of our need for and dependence on God.

Salt of the Earth

5TH SUNDAY IN ORDINARY TIME
Readings: Is 58:6-10, 1 Cor 2:1-5, Mt 5:13-16

Today's gospel follows immediately upon the beatitudes which begin the sermon on the mount. Jesus speaks directly to his disciples and calls them the salt of the earth and a light of the world. Their lives are no longer merely their own. What they do and are has implications for others, implications ultimately for the whole of humanity.

Salt gives flavor; it acts as a preservative. The presence in the world of people who have opened themselves to the gift of God's kingdom, and who try to live in ways that correspond to it and its values, makes a significant difference. Because of such people the world cannot but be a better place. They not only do good but help to keep the power of evil at bay.

It is not easy to be the salt of the earth. It is not easy always to act in a decent and moral and loving way, especially when such things are not valued by the culture in which one lives. It is here that Jesus' words challenge us. Just as salt can lose its flavor, so too can we cease to be in any decisive way his disciples. When we do, our lives lose their meaning and become of little value to anyone.

Light of the World

The Bible and the liturgy often have recourse to the image of light. At Christmas and Epiphany the coming of Jesus is likened to the dawning of a new day, to the sudden appearance in the midst of darkness of a great light. Here Jesus applies the image to us. We are to be a light of the world. We are not to hide who we are but to let it shine forth so that others, seeing us, will discern the light of life.

The image of light also figures in today's first reading. In a classic prophetic formulation, Isaiah reminds us that acts of ritual and devotion such as fasting must be accompanied by deeds of goodness and justice. What God asks of us is that we do the work of justice and peace, that we struggle against oppression and that we reach out a helping hand to those in need.

When we do what is right, when we feed the hungry and shelter the homeless and clothe the naked, our lives will be radiant like the dawn, brilliant like the noonday sun. We shall be a light in the world, and God will be with us. The more we do what is right, the more we can trust in God's help.

To Be a Sacrament

Jesus says that we should let our light shine before others so that they may see our good works and give glory to God. What is being suggested here is not simple. Ordinarily, as Jesus puts it elsewhere, it is better for the right hand not to know the good that the left hand does. We are so inclined to self-righteousness. And yet there is such a thing as false humility.

The saying of Jesus is analogous to what Vatican II meant when it spoke of the church as a sacrament. As a community of faith we are to be in the world a visible sign and an instrument of Christ's salvation. Our efforts to be people of faith and of love, people who care about the needy and about those who suffer, are carried by the gift of God's Spirit to us in Christ.

By sharing in the eucharist we proclaim our gratitude for God's gifts to us and express our continuing need for them. When we try to be good and loving it should be clear to everyone and especially to ourselves that our efforts are only possible because of what God has done for us.

The Power of God

A sense of radical dependence on God is at the heart of St. Paul's message and life. In today's second reading he insists that the success of his preaching in Corinth had nothing to do with human wisdom or human eloquence. It was a result of the power of the gospel itself and of the presence of the Spirit.

For Paul, no one finally has any reason to boast about his or her goodness. Salvation comes from God in Jesus Christ. Without God's sustaining and strengthening power we can do nothing of any lasting significance. In God and with God's help, however, we can do great things. We can live a life of holiness and justice and by doing so become witnesses to Jesus.

In his preaching of God's kingdom, Jesus offers us the possibility of a new beginning. Those who respond to him are to be the salt of the earth and a light for the world. No matter how intense the darkness or how bitter the unsavoriness of the times in which we happen to live, as disciples of Jesus we are to lead lives of goodness and love, of justice and mercy. Now as always, such lives make a difference.

To Fulfill the Law

6TH SUNDAY IN ORDINARY TIME
Readings: Sir 15:15-20, 1 Cor 2:6-10, Mt 5:17-37

Today's gospel, taken once again from the sermon on the mount, begins by enunciating a principle that must have been greatly cherished in Matthew's Jewish-Christian community. Jesus says that he came not to abolish the law or the prophets, but rather to bring them to their fulfillment. He is talking of the whole Jewish tradition, especially as it is formulated in the books of what we call the Old Testament.

The word "law" here translates the Hebrew word Torah. It refers primarily not to law in any narrow or legalistic sense, but to everything involved in God's covenant with Israel, including the concrete way of life that was to be a part of it. The Torah is also the name given to the first five books of the Bible, those in which the stories of creation and Abraham and the exodus figure so largely.

Although for Jews religion is above all a way of life, it is a way of life rooted in the creative and saving activity of God. The law is a gift of God and proclaims his fidelity even as it calls God's people to live in justice and goodness. Jesus came not to destroy such things but to renew and deepen them.

The "Antitheses"

The statement of principle is followed by a series of six contrast sayings, four of which are contained in our reading. In each of them Jesus refers to a teaching of the Torah and then adds by way of contrast, "but I say to you." The structure of the sayings has led people to describe them as "antitheses."

Where the Torah forbade murder and adultery, Jesus condemns anger and lust. His reasoning is clear. If murder is wrong, then so is anger, because it is in festering anger that violence and murder find a fertile ground. Jesus wants to make us think not just about evil actions but about the attitudes and the heart from which such actions come. Those who give in to anger, who insult others and call them names, are not all that distant from those who actually do violence.

Far from undermining or denying the Torah, such a view deepens and reinforces the positive thrust of what it proclaims. Nor is it, Jesus adds, enough simply to avoid negative sentiments. We need actively to seek reconciliation with all those with whom we are at odds.

Choose Life

Read with the gospel, today's first reading is enormously challenging. It emphasizes human freedom and responsibility. If we want to, it says, we can keep the commandments. Each and every one of us faces a choice, a choice between life and death. Nowhere has the way to true life been spelled out more dramatically, more forcefully, than in the sermon on the mount.

To understand how such a choice is possible, it is helpful to recall the context within which our reading from Sirach occurs. It has to do with God's gift of wisdom to those who fear him. The word "fear" here suggests a sense of God's holiness and at the same time an awareness of our weakness. It involves a turning to God in humility and a seeking of God's help.

The text describes wisdom as a mother or bride, as someone who welcomes and nourishes us. In the New Testament it is said that Jesus both teaches God's wisdom and embodies it. It is only by entrusting ourselves to him that we discover that his yoke is easy and his burden light.

God's Wisdom

Some of the same themes are echoed in today's second reading. Paul is reacting to the pretentiousness of some of the Corinthian Christians. They seem to have been rather arrogant about their "wisdom." He agrees that there is a Christian wisdom, but insists that it has nothing to do with the kind of worldly wisdom that their attitudes reveal.

God's wisdom is something hidden and secret, something that humans could never discover on their own. It is a wisdom that has been revealed in Christ and through the Spirit. For Paul the Spirit is the source of true wisdom. Whatever wisdom we have comes from the presence of God's Spirit in us.

To speak of God's wisdom is to speak of God's plan of salvation. God's intention from all eternity was to share his life with us. The manifestation of that intention in Christ fills us with hope. What God asks of us is that we love him and try to keep his commandments. If we do, we can look forward to something that goes beyond anything we can imagine — we can look forward to eternal life in God. That is our hope and our glory.

To Be Like God

7TH SUNDAY IN ORDINARY TIME
Readings: Lev 19:1-2, 17-18, 1 Cor 3:16-23, Mt 5:38-48

Once again today's gospel is taken from Matthew's account of the sermon on the mount. It contains the last two of the six sayings in which Jesus contrasts his understanding of God's will and of morality with traditional views. The section culminates in his challenge to us to be perfect as God is perfect.

The precept of "an eye for an eye and a tooth for a tooth," the so-called law of retaliation, was originally introduced to keep revenge within limits and thus to prevent a spiraling escalation of violence. For Jesus, however, such limitations are no longer enough. He wants us to repudiate not only acts of retaliation but even the desire for revenge. He would like to see us go beyond our natural tendency to bear grudges.

The examples he gives are enormously challenging. We are not to flinch when insulted, or to be less than generous when unreasonable demands are made of us. To the degree that we can, we are to respond to everyone who turns to us in need. If desires for revenge and retaliation often arise out of hurt pride, what Jesus asks presupposes a profound humility and a willingness to accept one's vulnerability. He seems to leave us without defenses in our dealings with one another.

Love Your Enemies

The second saying brings us to what is most central in Jesus' ethical teaching. We are to love not only our relatives and those who, in different ways, are near to us and good to us, but even those who hate us and who persecute us, those whom the world would spontaneously identify as our enemies.

To love those who love us, Jesus says, is not sufficient. It is in fact a relatively easy thing to do. What is challenging and requires effort is to reach out the hand of friendship or at least of acceptance to those who dislike us and think evil of us and who perhaps have even done harm to us. Any positive action here could well break through a pattern of animosity and begin to change the other person's attitude to us.

In justifying his call for universal love, Jesus appeals to the example of God who makes the sun rise and sends the rain on just and unjust alike. If we want truly to be God's children, then, insofar as it is possible for us, we must imitate God. We must, Jesus says, become perfect as God is perfect.

Be Holy, for God Is Holy

Today's first reading contains the opening verses and then a passage from near the end of chapter 19 of Leviticus. The whole chapter unfolds some of the implications of the remarkable saying with which it begins: "You shall be holy, for I the Lord your God am holy." The section omitted from our reading evokes the ten commandments, stressing in particular justice and mercy. It culminates in the command to "love your neighbor as yourself."

In the Bible the word holiness as applied to God has many meanings. Sometimes it points to what makes God utterly different from us and from the world. Holiness in this context is his divinity. Here, however, it has a moral meaning. To be holy is to be just and good, faithful and loving.

Whereas in Matthew Jesus asks us to be perfect as God is perfect, in Luke he speaks of mercy. Whether the reference is to holiness, perfection or mercy, the basic idea is the same. We are to be like God. For Jesus, what is most distinctive about God is universal love. To be like God is to love not only our friends but even those for whom we might naturally feel aversion.

We Belong to Christ

The ideal presented by Jesus in the sermon on the mount is beyond our capacity. If we look only at ourselves and our natural inclinations and at the way we react to the appearance of sudden and unpleasant demands in our lives, we recognize how far above us is its vision of generosity and self-forgetfulness.

Today's second reading suggests how such an ideal might become a reality. Paul says that we are holy, not because we have already become morally perfect, but because God has made us holy by giving us a share in his Spirit. The presence of God's Spirit in us makes us God's temple, the place where God dwells.

Because of the Spirit we belong to Christ and share in some way in his life. The ideal of the sermon on the mount is not an abstraction. It is in many ways a description of the actual life that Jesus lived. That which alone can make such a life possible for us is the presence of Christ's Spirit in us. His Spirit is a Spirit of holiness and, if we cooperate, it will gradually transform us from within until our lives reflect the holiness of God.

The Child of Her Womb

8TH SUNDAY IN ORDINARY TIME
Readings: Is 49:13-15, 1 Cor 4:1-5, Mt 6:24-34

Today's gospel, as that of the last several weeks, is taken from Matthew's account of the sermon on the mount. Although our text is made up of a number of somewhat disparate sayings, its dominant theme is clearly that of trust in God and in God's provident care for us. We are encouraged not to worry about food or clothing but to be confident that God will see to our needs. Jesus points to the lilies of the fields and the birds of the air and argues that because of our unique value in God's eyes he will take even greater care of us than he does of them.

At first view, what Jesus says seems to stand in stark contrast to our own experience of life. The widespread existence of such things as unemployment, competition, rising costs, and social violence makes it difficult to see how we could ever arrive at the kind of detachment and indifference that Jesus seems to be suggesting. As true as this is of us as individuals, it is all the more the case when we have to be concerned for our families as well. And yet even as we think this way, we recognize that there is something in what Jesus says that touches a responsive chord within us.

Loving Father, Tender Mother

The text reveals a great deal about Jesus' own religious attitude. The God on whom his human identity was totally focused was experienced as a loving father. The phrase "heavenly Father" comes back twice in the present passage. The word expresses the utter trust and love that was at the heart of Jesus' relationship with God.

The conviction that God is someone who cares for and who intervenes on behalf of people is central to the whole Bible. In

61

order to express this conviction biblical writers use many and varied images. God is our rock and fortress, our shepherd and guide. In today's first reading God is compared to a mother giving birth to and nursing her child. In thinking of God we need to have recourse to maternal as well as paternal language.

To those who fear that God might forget them, the prophet asks whether a mother could ever forget or fail to have compassion on the child that she bore in her womb and nursed at her breast. Such is God's love and concern for us. In fact it is even greater. While we have to admit the possibility that a human mother might forget, God will never forget.

Seek First the Kingdom

If Jesus insists on the gracious reality of God, he is in no sense encouraging irresponsibility on our part. The sayings about trust are framed by two invitations to discipleship. No one, Jesus says, can serve two masters. We cannot give ourselves totally to both God and mammon, God and wealth, God and anything that is not God. The passage ends with a challenge to commit ourselves to the kingdom of God and to the goodness, justice, and love that are so much a part of it.

In Jesus' own case the way of trust led to persecution, misunderstanding, betrayal, and death. On the cross he seems to have been overwhelmed by a sense of abandonment. Through it all he entered in the most radical way imaginable into the kind of human experiences that threaten to belie the attitude and stance to which he invites us. And yet he never gave up his sense of God's tender and loving presence in his life.

Servants of Christ

In writing to the Corinthians Paul addresses the nature of his vocation and responsibility as an apostle. Questions have been raised about his activity and about his relation to other Christian preachers. Paul insists on the secondary and relative role of all ministers of the gospel. It is God finally who calls people to faith and who gives them the gift of the Spirit.

In today's passage Paul asks his readers to think of him as a servant of Christ and as a steward of God's mysteries. The phrase has often been applied to the Christian priesthood. People, whether lay or ordained, who exercise any kind of leadership or ministry in the church do so not in their own name but in the name of Christ. What they offer is not their own wisdom but that of God. Their success depends on God.

Paul ends with an affirmation of hope. Although he recognizes his own weaknesses and inadequacies, he does not judge himself nor does he worry about the judgment of others. He knows that our lives are in the hands of God. At the end of time God will reveal their true meaning and in doing so will fulfill our hope and justify our trust.

Lent

Christian and Adam

1ST SUNDAY OF LENT
Readings: Gen 2:7-9, 16-18, 25; 3:1-7, Rom 5:12-19, Mt 4:1-11

The liturgical season of Lent is above all a period of preparation for the solemn celebration at Easter of the death and resurrection of Jesus. The paschal mystery, as it is called, is at the heart of our faith. In and through it God reconciled us to himself and offered us the possibility of a new life.

From an early date, Easter was associated with baptism, the ritual in which initially individuals are brought into contact with the saving power of Jesus' death and resurrection. The fact that the liturgy invites us to renew our baptismal promises at Easter suggests that Lent should be seen as a time to reflect seriously on baptism and on its implications for life.

Although originally a much shorter period, Lent eventually came to embrace forty days in memory of Jesus' forty days in the desert prior to the beginning of his public life. Those forty days, as today's gospel reminds us, were a time of prayer and fasting and of temptation or testing. They are reminiscent of the forty year period that Israel wandered in the wilderness before entering the promised land.

The Son of God

To the temptations of the devil Jesus responds by quoting scripture. All three passages are from a speech by Moses in Deuteronomy, chapters 6 to 8. In using these specific texts Jesus wants to relate his mission and ministry to the story of Israel. Just as it was tested in regard to its fidelity at that time, so is he being tested now.

In the background of Deuteronomy is the theme of the

covenant. In calling the people out of Egypt, God entered into an agreement, a covenant with them. He made them his people and promised them his love and support. They, for their part, had to commit themselves to him and to the way of life implied in the commandments. They were to live as his people.

The devil tests Jesus in order to see whether and in what sense he is God's Son, God's faithful servant. The temptations reach a climax in the third one in which Jesus is offered dominion over the whole world if only he will adore the tempter. His response is decisive: God alone is to be worshiped and served. Beyond that nothing more need be said.

To Be Like God

The temptations all turn in different ways on God's will and on Jesus' attitude to it. As important as nourishment is, human beings cannot live by bread alone. We are spiritual beings with a relationship to God. The food that we need to foster that relationship is the word that comes from the mouth of God.

Our faith in God, however, does not mean that we can "tempt" God, that we can decide what God should or should not do for us or for the world and then, by implication, sit back in judgment on him if he fails to do what we expect. We belong to God, not God to us. We are to seek to do his will, not he ours.

The attitude of Jesus in the gospel is dramatically different from that of Adam and Eve evoked in our first reading. Although made by God and given all the gifts of creation, they are not satisfied. They refuse to accept the limits that are theirs as creatures and want to become like God. Their arrogance leads to their destruction. They lose their innocence and God's friendship and become prey to violence and death.

The Obedience of One Person

In today's second reading Paul relates and contrasts Adam and Christ. We are all children of the first parents, heirs both of their dignity as creatures made in God's image and likeness and of the tragedy of their sin. Through them, Paul says, sin has come into the world, and with sin death. Their rebellion against God changed the human condition for all time.

Paul's interest, however, is not so much in Adam and Eve as in Christ. He marks the beginning of a new and renewed humanity. Through him and through his obedience to God, the ravages of sin are overcome. Death gives way to the promise of a new life. If by our very existence as human beings we share in the self-destructiveness of Adam and Eve, by faith we are one with Christ.

Jesus is the Son of God who came to do God's will and thus end the reign of sin and death. The testing in the wilderness at the beginning of his public life reveals his true character. His fidelity in the face of rejection and the cross will seal his mission and win for us forgiveness and reconciliation. Baptism offers us a share in his life even as it demands from us a special effort to be one with him in his obedience to God.

Listen to Him

2ND SUNDAY OF LENT
Readings: Gen 12:1-4, 2 Tim 1:8b-10, Mt 17:1-9

In the lives of the disciples the transfiguration represents one of those privileged moments when suddenly everything becomes clear. Jesus invites three of his closest associates to withdraw for a time with him from whatever it is they are doing. He leads them up what is here described as a mountain, a favored place in the biblical tradition for an encounter with God.

The account of what happens to Jesus suggests what after the resurrection will be called his glorification. His face becomes like the sun and his clothes dazzling white. Although still very much himself, the earthly limitations that he shares with us have fallen away. He is as we all hope to become once we have entered into the presence of the beauty and the glory of God.

The appearance of Moses and Elijah evokes the whole religious history of Israel and in particular the role in it of the law and the prophets. They are here to bear witness to Jesus and to the fact that in him God's saving activity among the people has reached a new and definitive stage. The glorified Jesus embodies the goal of human history and of all of God's creation.

Do Not Be Afraid

The reaction of Peter is intriguing. It is almost as if he wants to take hold of the moment and to give it some kind of permanence. He proposes setting up three tents, one for Jesus, one for Moses and one for Elijah. Before anyone can respond, however, the voice of God is heard. It proclaims Jesus as the beloved Son to whom they are to listen.

The experience of God can take many forms and provoke a wide range of responses. The more direct and intense it is, the more people tend to react with awe and fear. That is what happens here. Jesus, however, reassures the disciples. He is still with them. The vision is meant to strengthen them and to help them understand and therefore deal with what lies ahead.

Daily life continues, and for Jesus it will soon bring suffering and rejection. For his followers, it will entail doubt and denial and the temptation to despair. When Jesus tells Peter and the others not to be afraid, he is obviously referring to the present moment but he is also looking ahead to the challenges that they will soon have to face.

The Story of Salvation

Chapter 12 of Genesis from which our first reading is taken marks a new moment in the story of God's dealings with humankind. Abraham is regarded in the Bible as the first of the patriarchs, the one from whom the Jewish people will eventually spring. The God who appears to Moses in the burning bush will identify himself as the God of Abraham and Isaac and Jacob. Abraham remains for Christians as well as Jews "our father in faith."

The story of Abraham and Sarah is the story of a couple called by God to leave their country and to set out on a journey for an unknown land. God promises to make of them a mighty nation, a people whose destiny will be tied up with the salvation of the world. What God asks of them more than anything else is faith and trust. He promises to be with them along the path that he has called them to walk. The divine plan begun in Abraham is carried forward with Moses and with all the prophets and other great figures who follow him. The coming of Jesus reaffirms God's saving intent and brings it to an initial climax.

Called with a Holy Calling

Today's second reading evokes in more general terms what is suggested in the other readings by the mention of Abraham and Moses and Elijah. God, it says, had a purpose for us from before the beginning of time. The purpose has been revealed in Jesus Christ. It has to do with the overcoming of all that is evil and destructive, including death itself. Put more positively, God's purpose for us is life and immortality.

What the transfiguration was for the disciples, the whole life of Jesus is for us. In Jesus, God's intent for humankind is revealed. Having come from God, we will one day be brought home to God. When that happens we will be one in glory with Christ.

Truly to celebrate the eucharist is to withdraw for a moment from everyday life and to become aware of its deeper meaning and of God's purpose in regard to it. The eucharist reminds us of, and renders present among us, the self-giving love of Jesus. In doing so it catches us up with him as he comes in perfect adoration before God. Here we are able to realize something of what is involved in being members of Christ's body. Nourished and encouraged, we take up again the challenges of everyday life.

Living Water

3RD SUNDAY OF LENT
Readings: Ex 17:3-7, Rom 5:1-2, 5-8, Jn 4:5-42

The account in John's gospel of the encounter between Jesus and the Samaritan woman is one of the best known and most beautifully written passages in the entire New Testament. John's artistry transforms what might have been the simple report of an isolated incident into a theological reflection on, and proclamation of, the deep meaning of the life and ministry of Jesus.

The disciples were surprised that Jesus was talking with a woman. She, for her part, wondered that he, a Jew, would want to have anything to do with a Samaritan like herself. For Jesus, however, no limits are to be put on the gift that God is offering through him. If, in God's providence, salvation comes from the Jews, it is ultimately meant for everyone.

The beginning of the dialogue could hardly be more simple. Jesus asks the woman at the well for some water to drink. As the conversation moves on he tells her that if she knew who he was, she would ask him for a drink and he would give her living water, water that would spring up within her to eternal life. Water has here become a symbol of the life-giving gift that Jesus offers.

Spirit and Truth

In the Bible and among at least some Jews in the time of Jesus, water was used to suggest divine wisdom and more particularly the Torah, the law given through Moses. Against this background, the water Jesus offers is clearly God's revelation, God's truth. Jesus not only speaks God's word, he is the Word incarnate. He is the revelation of God in person.

The use of water as a symbol of the life-giving presence of God's Spirit is also common in the Old Testament. John's gospel had already drawn the two realities together in its account of the conversation between Jesus and Nicodemus: "No one can enter the kingdom of God without being born of water and Spirit." The Spirit in our hearts will lead us to eternal life.

The theme of Spirit and truth becomes explicit in the exchange between Jesus and the woman in regard to where and how God wants us to worship him. True worship, Jesus says, will no longer be restricted to any particular place but will be distinguished by the fact that it takes place in the Spirit and in truth. Through the gift of the Spirit people will become one with Jesus in his worship of the Father.

The Savior of the World

The story draws to a climax in the deepening recognition by the woman of who Jesus is. His knowledge of her personal life makes her initially think of him as a prophet. As he talks about the nature of true worship, she begins to wonder whether he is the messiah. His answer is clear: "I am he." The phrase points to the radical unity of Jesus with the Father, the one who revealed himself to Moses in the burning bush as "He who is."

The report of the woman to the townspeople brings them out to see for themselves who this Jesus is. They are moved by what he says and come to believe in him, now not because of anything the woman has told them, but because they personally have come to recognize that Jesus is "the Savior of the world."

Paul proclaims the same truth, although in different language, in our second reading. It is through Jesus Christ, he says, that we are justified and obtain peace before God. We know that God loves us because Christ died for us. Through the gift of Christ's Spirit, God has poured his love into our hearts.

Faith, Hope and Love

Today's brief reading from the letter to the Romans summarizes much of what Paul himself had experienced and believed and had come to understand as being at the very heart of the gospel. Salvation begins with God and with God's love.

Jesus comes from God. His human love and self-giving are rooted in and manifest God's love for us. Through the death and resurrection of Jesus God has reconciled us and given us the gift of the Spirit.

Paul likes to describe our passage from death to life, from sin to friendship with God, as a process of justification. It means being declared and being made just or upright before God. Because it is God who justifies us in Christ, we have no cause to boast. We are justified not by our efforts, but by God's gift.

The love of God that Paul says is poured into our hearts by the gift of the Spirit is meant to bear fruit. This is something with which we need to cooperate. As we struggle to do so, it is important to remember that we are not alone. The Spirit is with us, giving us the hope that what God has begun he will bring to fulfillment. We live "in hope of sharing the glory of God."

Light of the World

4TH SUNDAY OF LENT
Readings: 1 Sam 16:1b, 6-7, 10-13a, Eph 5:8-14, Jn 9:1-41

As important as the cure of the man born blind is in today's gospel, it is clearly secondary to the account of his gradual coming to faith in Jesus. As so often with John, a physical healing points to a deeper spiritual reality. The miracles Jesus works are to be read by us as signs of what God, in and through him, continues to offer to us today.

The unfolding of the miracle is briefly although colorfully told. Jesus mixes saliva and dirt to create a paste which he applies to the blind man's eyes. He then sends him to wash in a nearby pool, and when the man does he discovers that he is able to see. The event provokes astonishment among people who knew about his blindness and attracts the attention of a group of Pharisees.

The heart of the story is the exchange that takes place between the cured man and the Pharisees. As the conversation progresses, his sense of the mystery of the person of Jesus deepens and his faith becomes more explicit. The Pharisees, on the other hand, become more and more convinced that Jesus is a sinner, someone who in spite of appearances cannot possibly be doing the work of God.

A Man from God

When first asked about his cure, the man refers simply to "the man Jesus" and to what he did. In response to the questioning of the Pharisees, however, he goes a step further and calls Jesus a prophet. This seems to provoke them, and they begin to wonder whether the man had been born blind at all.

Initially the Pharisees are torn. The miracle, if it really took place, is a sign that God is with Jesus. The fact, however, that in performing it Jesus disregarded the sabbath is a scandal. Eventually this begins to loom so large that it blinds them to the good that Jesus is doing."This man," they say, "is a sinner." Someone who breaks the law cannot be from God.

The man is not persuaded by their argument. His reasoning is simple and clear. A cure like his can only be done with the help of God. If Jesus does the works of God, then Jesus himself must come from God. The reaction of the Pharisees is typical of those of us who for whatever reason do not want to believe. At their wits' end, they drive the man from their presence.

I Came for Judgment

The climax of the story is the encounter between Jesus and the former blind man. When Jesus reveals himself as the one who had cured him, the man confesses his faith without hesitation and bows down in worship. His healing is now complete. He sees not only with his eyes but with his heart and soul as well. He sees with the eyes of faith.

Jesus says that he came into the world in order that people might see, that they might see the truth about themselves and above all about God and about God's intentions in regard to human life. Jesus reveals God; he is the true light who is capable of enlightening everyone who turns to him. For those, however, who refuse to accept him, those who shut themselves up in their own blindness and do not allow him to heal them, his coming involves a judgment. The greatest tragedy is not physical but spiritual blindness. Those who obstinately identify their blindness with sight will never know their need for Jesus.

Light in the Lord

The fact that the name of the pool to which the blind man was sent to wash was called Siloam, a word meaning "sent," led the early church to recognize in the story a reference to baptism. Jesus is the one who is sent by the Father. To be baptized in him is to receive the gift of spiritual insight.

The themes of baptism and light are also present in today's second reading. Paul tells us that although we were once darkness, we are now light in the Lord. The last verse may well be from an early baptismal hymn. "Sleeper, awake! Rise from the dead, and Christ will shine on you." To be without Christ is to be in the darkness of death. Through baptism into Christ, his radiance shines on us and brings us light and life.

If we are light, Paul says, then we must live as children of light. Our lives must correspond to the new life that is ours through baptism. The text speaks of doing what is good and right and true. The gospels emphasize the importance of imitating Jesus and of keeping his commandments. The Easter liturgy proclaims Christ as the light and, in doing so, welcomes the newly baptized and invites all of us to reaffirm our faith in him and to renew our commitment to live in ways that reflect his light.

I Am the Resurrection

5TH SUNDAY OF LENT
Readings: Ezek 37:12-14, Rom 8:8-11, Jn 11:1-45

In the story of the raising of Lazarus, as so often in John's gospel, the miracle that Jesus works is presented as a sign pointing to and illustrating the meaning of his life and destiny. The actual account of the miracle is relatively brief and comes at the end of a rather complicated narrative in which Jesus suggests the significance of what is to happen in his conversations with the disciples and with Martha and Mary.

For many today, one of the more touching aspects of the account is its insistence on the love that Jesus had for Lazarus and his sisters. The evangelist comments on it at the beginning, as do those who see Jesus weeping near the tomb. Lazarus is identified by his sisters simply as the one whom Jesus loves. At a deeper level, the phrase applies to each of us.

The dialogue that takes place between Jesus and the disciples introduces a number of key themes. Lazarus' illness will not lead to death but to a manifestation of God's glory, God's power and goodness. Jesus himself will be glorified and will be revealed once again as the Son of God. The miracle as a true sign will deepen the faith of the disciples.

Death and Life

Unlike the other gospel writers who focus on Jesus' preaching of the kingdom of God, John emphasizes the importance of Jesus himself. It is Jesus who in all that he says and does reveals the Father and who offers us the gift of eternal life. Faith, for John, is above all faith in Jesus and in the gracious God who sent him and who works through him.

In John's gospel Jesus is presented in turn as the bread of

life, as a source of living water, as the light of the world, as the true vine of which we are the branches. In today's reading Jesus identifies himself as the resurrection and the life. All these different formulations focus our attention on Jesus and on the gifts that God is offering us through him.

The words resurrection and life clearly go together. Jesus is the resurrection because of the hope which he offers to all who believe in him. He is the life because he is the source of that new life that one day will flower into eternal life. Those who believe in Jesus share in that life even now. Although they will die a physical death, they will never die spiritually.

God's Glory Revealed

In spite of Martha's proclamation of faith in Jesus as the messiah and Son of God, she hesitates when he asks that the stone be removed from the tomb. As profound as her faith already is, it still needs to be deepened. Jesus prays that everyone will understand that it is God who is about to manifest his glory and in seeing it will believe in him as the one sent by God.

Today's first reading concludes the famous passage in Ezekiel where the prophet describes a vision in which God raises up dry bones and covers them with flesh and breathes into them the breath of life. For the Jews, their exile in Babylon was a form of death. Defeated and driven into a foreign land, they despaired of their life as God's people. The prophet assures them that in spite of all that has happened God has not abandoned them. He will raise them up and fill them with his Spirit and bring them back to their own land. The biblical God is a God not of death but of life.

The Spirit of Life

If Jesus in his preaching, miracles and final destiny was the resurrection and the life present in the world, he continues to be that for us today through the power of the Spirit. In our second reading Paul relates the theme of life and of resurrection to the Spirit as well as to Jesus.

For us the Spirit is the Spirit both of God and of the risen

Christ. By the gift of the Spirit we belong to Jesus and share his life. In that sense the Spirit is for us the Spirit of life. Paul says that it was the Spirit who raised Jesus from the dead. We have therefore every reason to hope that the same Spirit will one day raise us to eternal life with Christ.

Easter celebrates the resurrection of Jesus, the coming home of Jesus in the fullness of his humanity to the God from whom and for whom he lived and died. Our celebration of Jesus' triumph is at the same time a celebration of the gift of life he came to share with us, a gift that most of first received in baptism. It is a celebration, too, of the hope we have of one day being brought by the power of the Spirit to share in fullness in the risen life of Christ.

Faithful unto Death

PASSION (PALM) SUNDAY
**Readings: Mt 21:1-11, Is 50:4-7, Phil 2:6-11,
Mt 26:14-27, 66**

Today's liturgy begins by recalling the triumphant entry of
Jesus into Jerusalem. People, touched by his preaching and activity, welcome him enthusiastically into the holy city. They strew
cloaks and branches before him and greet him with shouts of
Hosanna and with the words of a psalm: "Blessed is the one who
comes in the name of the Lord."

The contrast between this scene and the account of the passion and death in today's gospel could hardly be more dramatic.
We seem to go from one emotional extreme to the other. Welcome
and triumph are transformed into rejection and failure. And yet
there is no real contradiction. The only reason we continue to proclaim the story of Christ's suffering is that we know that it is the
prelude to the resurrection.

The account of the passion that we read today is from
Matthew. Although very similar to that of Mark, it emphasizes
how what is taking place fulfills the scriptures. Nothing that happens is purely arbitrary. Matthew also underlines the fact that
Jesus, in spite of what is done to him, remains the master of his
destiny. He embraces it in obedience and fidelity to God.

Your Will Be Done

The attitude of Jesus in regard to what is happening is perhaps best reflected by his prayer in the garden of Gethsemani. At
the last supper Jesus had entrusted to his disciples the gift of the
eucharist and with it the meaning of his life and death. He came
to bring forgiveness and to seal a new covenant between God and
humankind. In the garden Jesus confronts what lies before him.

He prays, as we would pray, that he might be spared from pain and suffering. Even as he asks this, however, he makes clear that his deepest desire is to do God's will. He is ready to accept whatever has to be accepted in the fulfillment of the mission that has been entrusted to him.

Over the centuries Christians have been struck by the extent and depth of Jesus' suffering. As important as it is, however, in all its details, what is even more significant is the attitude with which he approached it. Suffering of itself is not redemptive. The key to Jesus' whole life was his sense of mission. He came to do God's will. Nothing, not even suffering, pain, and death, will deflect him from this.

Betrayed and Recognized

In addition to the physical pain involved in the passion, it is striking to reflect on the degree to which Jesus was betrayed and abandoned. As incomprehensible as the action of Judas was, it stands for the betrayal involved in all our sins. Peter, the rock, reveals his cowardice and lack of commitment. With the arrest, "all the disciples deserted him and fled." The only ones who stayed, according to Matthew, were some women.

If this is the treatment that Jesus received from his friends and followers, it is not surprising to see that others treated him in an even worse manner. The Roman soldiers made fun of and abused him; the passersby laughed at him; those involved in his condemnation mocked him for his trust in God.

The cry of Jesus, "My God, my God, why have you abandoned me?" suggests the depth of his loneliness. That cry, however, begins Psalm 22, a lamentation in which a person pours out his anguish but in which finally he comes to a statement of trust in God's saving power. The death of Jesus provokes from the Roman soldiers an act of faith: "Truly this man was God's Son."

He Emptied Himself

Today's second reading offers a theological reflection on Jesus' death. In Jesus the Word of God, the eternal Son of God took on human form. In embracing a human life, God made his own our destiny. Paul sees this coming of God among us as an extraordinary act of divine self-emptying. If this is already true of the simple fact of the incarnation, it is even more true of Jesus' willingness, in fulfillment of his mission, to undergo the terrible pain and suffering of his passion and death. The self-emptying of God in taking on human form is echoed and becomes tangible in the humility and self-giving of Jesus.

Because Jesus was faithful to the end, Paul says, God exalted him on high, raised him to the fullness of life, and gave him a share in the divine name itself. The passion and death of Jesus is more than the story of one more innocent and good man crushed by the evil of the world. It is the manifestation of God's infinite love for us. The cross was for Jesus and is for us a threshold that opens onto the glory of God.

Easter and the Easter Season

Christis Risen

EASTER SUNDAY
Readings: Acts 10:34a, 36-43, Col 3:1-4 or 1 Cor 5:6b-8, Jn 20:1-18

Easter is a time of joy and of hope. Its message speaks of life and of renewal. Jesus who died on the cross has been raised by God to the fullness of life. In his case, death did not have the last word. He lives, he lives with God, he lives for us. What seemed initially to the disciples to be utter defeat and failure was transformed on Easter morning into triumph and glory.

Each of the gospels tells the story and proclaims the truth of Easter in its own distinctive way. In today's reading John insists on the significance of the beloved disciple and on the special role of Mary Magdalene. It is Mary who first discovers the empty tomb and who tells Peter and the other disciple about it. When they come to the tomb Peter is perplexed, while the beloved disciple immediately believes.

In John's gospel, the disciple whom Jesus loved, the disciple traditionally identified with John, seems to embody the ideal of true discipleship. While we are told that Jesus had a special love for him, the implication is that the love was reciprocated. Love alone can provide the mind and heart that make faith in the resurrection possible.

Apostle to the Apostles

The account of the meeting between Mary Magdalene and Jesus says a great deal about the meaning of the resurrection. Having stayed behind and still not understanding what has happened, Mary weeps. She weeps not only for the death of Jesus but also because the body that she has come to honor has disappeared. Meeting Jesus, she recognizes him only when he says her name.

The words of Jesus are somewhat mysterious. He tells Mary not to hold on to him, not to cling to him, because he has not yet ascended to the Father. The resurrection is not a return of Jesus to this life, nor is it a taking up in the same form of relationships that once existed. It marks a new beginning. Once glorified, Jesus will be present to believers through the Spirit.

Mary is to tell the disciples that Jesus must first ascend "to his Father and your Father, to his God and your God." Believers are to become sisters and brothers of Jesus and to share in his relation with God. Because of her role in proclaiming this to the disciples, the medieval tradition came to bestow on Mary the title "apostle to the apostles."

Our Paschal Lamb

The resurrection of Jesus is inseparable from his life and especially from his death. It affirms the truth and the value of all that he said and did. His preaching of the nearness of God's kingdom and of the possibility of forgiveness and of new life has now been fulfilled in the most unexpected of ways.

Paul compares the death and resurrection of Jesus to the Passover, to the liberating activity of God in saving Israel out of slavery in Egypt. Christ, Paul says, is our paschal sacrifice. His self-giving even unto death has become for us a means of reconciliation with God and of liberation from sin and death.

Easter proclaims that God exists and that he is on the side of life and of goodness. In bringing Jesus through death to life, God reveals his active concern for and involvement in our history. He calls us to identify with him in furthering what contributes to life and in struggling against all that would undermine it. Such activity will never be in vain. Our final destiny is eternal fulfillment with Christ in God.

Baptized in Christ

Easter and baptism belong together because it is through faith and baptism that we are brought for the first time into contact with the power for life of Christ's death and resurrection. To be baptized is to be plunged into the death of Jesus so that we may live with him in newness of life.

Today's reading from Colossians insists that in some way we have already been raised with Christ and share his life. Putting it even more dramatically, it affirms that Christ is our life. Such formulations point to what is most central in our religion. Through Christ and the Spirit, God calls us to share his life and to experience the most intimate of relationships with him. In the words of Jesus, he is our Father and our God.

Our annual celebration of Easter is an occasion to renew faith and deepen commitment. In repeating our baptismal promises, we both recall what was done for us in the past and renew our dedication. Christ lives. He lives with God, and through the Spirit he lives with us. The joy and hope and love that ought to mark the lives of believers give witness to the resurrection.

Life in His Name

2ND SUNDAY OF EASTER
Readings: Acts 2:42-47, 1 Pet 1:3-9, Jn 20:19-31

A central theme in today's readings is faith: faith in the risen Christ, faith in the salvation that comes from God through him. The gospel continues John's account of the first Easter. The risen Jesus appears to the disciples who recognize and believe in him. In a gesture reminiscent of the creation of Adam, he breathes out the Holy Spirit on them and commissions them to carry on his mission of forgiveness and reconciliation.

Thomas, one of the twelve, was not there to share this experience with the others, and when told about it he refused to believe on the basis of their testimony. He announces that he will accept what they are saying only if he can put his finger in the mark of the nails and his hand in Christ's side. His is the attitude of rational and skeptical humanity. He wants to establish his own conditions for believing.

When Thomas eventually encounters Jesus, his doubts vanish. His cry of faith marks a highpoint in the entire New Testament. He recognizes Jesus as both Lord and God. The risen Christ has been so transformed by the glory of God that to the eyes of faith he shares forever the reality and the name of God.

Those Who Have Not Seen

If today's gospel is primarily about the coming to faith of the original disciples, its ending points to the future and to those who, like us, will one day believe on the basis of their word. In response to Thomas, Jesus declares blessed those who have not seen but who yet will come to faith.

The evangelist rounds off what he has said about the appearances of the risen Christ with a word of explanation of why he has written the things that he has. It is so that people might come to believe in Jesus as the messiah or Christ and as the Son of God and by believing have life in his name.

In all its parts the New Testament teaches that faith is the fundamental condition for receiving the salvation that God offers in Christ. We need to believe that God in his graciousness and mercy has turned to us in the life, teaching and destiny of Jesus. For John, faith focuses in a special way on Jesus himself. He reveals God and brings to us the gift of eternal life. Faith in him is inseparable from faith in God's presence in him and from faith in the new life to which we are called.

A Living Hope

The reading from 1 Peter picks up and reinforces the same themes. The resurrection of Jesus is a saving event. In raising Jesus from the dead, God has given us the possibility of a new birth. Through faith we die to what is destructive and sinful in ourselves and rise to a life the final fulfillment of which is now hidden in God but which one day will be revealed in Christ.

The people to whom Peter writes are undergoing some difficulty, perhaps a persecution. His message to them is one of hope. Present trials can be seen as occasions for deepening and purifying faith. Faith is not something that comes all at once or that is self-evident. It involves growth and the ongoing effort to live its implications.

Peter seems to be speaking directly of us when he says that although we have not seen Christ we love him and believe in him. In our Easter celebrations we are filled with joy as we recall his triumph and reflect on the salvation that one day we will share with him. Peace, hope and joy are the all but inevitable fruit of the Easter faith.

A Community of Faith

Christian faith involves us not only with Christ but with one another. The reading from Acts describes how the first believers came together to form a community of faith. They knew that faith had implications for life and especially for the way they were to treat one another. In their enthusiasm, they put their possessions in common so that all could benefit from them.

The life of the early church is said to have been marked by four things: the apostles' teaching, fellowship, the breaking of bread and prayer. Faith needs to be nourished by the word of God and by efforts of church leaders to apply its teaching to changing situations. The word fellowship or communion points to the love and mutual service that help to define discipleship.

The reference to prayer and to the breaking of the bread or the eucharist underlines the need that faith has to express itself in praise and worship. To pray is to be aware of and to become open to God's presence in our lives. Prayer and service are the necessary conditions for a life of faith.

Recognizing Jesus

3RD SUNDAY OF EASTER
Readings: Acts 2:14, 22b-28, 1 Pet 1:17-21, Lk 24:13-35

The story of the encounter of the two disciples with Jesus on the road to Emmaus is one of the most dramatically formulated and moving of the various gospel accounts of the Easter experience. It is a story with which we can easily identify. Nothing is more natural than to think of life as a journey. All of us, at times, walk in despair; all of us are invited to become aware of the presence of Jesus with us.

Initially the disciples fail to recognize the stranger who has engaged them in conversation. There is something about him, however, that draws them out. They tell him about what has happened and about the hopes that Jesus had awakened in so many. The despair that his death provoked is eloquently evoked in the phrase: "We had hoped that he was the one to redeem Israel."

The disciples go on to say that they have heard about the women going to the tomb and discovering that the body had disappeared. They do not know what to make of the report that angels had announced that Jesus was alive. It is at this point that the stranger begins to interpret the scriptures and to show them that the messiah had to suffer before being glorified.

The Breaking of Bread

Meals play a surprisingly important role in the gospel story. When Jesus eats with publicans and sinners, with the poor and with outcasts, he announces by what he is doing that such people are called to the kingdom of God. To share a meal with others is in some way to enter into communion with them.

The disciples invite the stranger to share their meal. When, in the course of it, he takes bread, says the blessing and gives it to them, they recognize who he is. The phrase "the breaking of bread" was widely used in the early church to refer to the eucharist. The Emmaus story announces that the risen Jesus can be encountered in the ritual re-enactment of the last supper. In the eucharist Jesus continues to be the host sharing himself in the form of food with those who approach his table.

Having recognized Jesus, the disciples reflect back on their experience and realize how deeply they had already been touched as he interpreted the scriptures for them. They sensed something special in what was happening. The implication is clear: the risen Jesus remains among us in word as well as in sacrament.

God of the Living

The excerpt from Peter's Pentecost sermon that constitutes today's first reading offers an example of how the disciples used what we have come to call the Old Testament to help them understand and proclaim Jesus and his meaning for us. The psalmist expresses total trust in God. God's presence will protect him from corruption and lead him on the path of life.

In the second reading Peter encourages his readers to continue to live in trust. In raising Jesus from the dead God has revealed that he is a God of the living, a God of life and of salvation. That he is also our God gives us hope that our lives have a meaning and are being directed to a goal.

Faith in God brings into our hearts what Peter describes as a "reverent fear." It makes us realize something of the seriousness of life. It also affirms our extraordinary dignity. God cares about us and in Christ has saved us from sin and self-destructiveness. Our destiny is to share Jesus' risen life.

Jesus Lives

The resurrection marks a decisive turning point in the life of Jesus but also in his relationship to us. Faith in the resurrection affirms that the humanity of Jesus has entered once and for all into the sphere of God, thus taking on eternal validity. The resurrection is not the abandonment by the Word of the human life that he had embraced in the incarnation but rather the bringing of it to its definitive fulfillment.

If Jesus is alive in God, then his triumph has implications for us. The resurrection marks the beginning of a new manner of Jesus' presence among us. As the risen Christ, he is present in and through the Spirit. Beginning with the resurrection, Christ and the Spirit have become inseparable. For Christian believers the Spirit is the Spirit both of God and of the risen Jesus.

The path of life takes many turns. Sometimes we walk in darkness, sometimes in light. Whatever our situation, the Easter message reminds us, Christ is alive and with us. The scriptures and the eucharist offer privileged moments in which we can encounter him. They remind us at the same time that he is always with us and perhaps especially in moments of despair.

Eternal Shepherd

4TH SUNDAY OF EASTER
Readings: Acts 2:14a, 36b-41, 1 Pet 2:20b-25, Jn 10:1-10

Today's gospel contains the first part of a rather long sermon or discourse of Jesus in which he recounts a parable and then offers an explanation of it. The parable weaves together a number of traditional biblical images: shepherd and sheep, a sheepfold and the gate that opens onto it. Although Jesus identifies himself as both the gate and the shepherd, what he says about the latter is omitted from our text.

The parable evokes several themes. Jesus contrasts the true shepherd with those whom he describes as thieves and bandits. They do not enter in by the gate but by some other and devious way. The shepherd, by contrast, acts publicly and in the light; he is known by gatekeeper and sheep alike. He calls his sheep by name and they follow him.

As the gate, Jesus is the one through whom we are to pass if we want to find nourishment and safekeeping. The image is reminiscent of another phrase in John's gospel: "I am the way, the truth and the life." Jesus reveals God, brings from God a gift of life, is the mediator, the bridge, the gate, the way by which God and God's gifts come to us and we return to God.

Lord and Messiah

All of today's readings affirm in different ways the unique role that Jesus continues to play in our lives. The text from Acts contains the conclusion of Peter's Pentecost sermon. His basic message is summed up in the affirmation that God has raised up the crucified Jesus and made him both Lord and messiah. All appearances to the contrary, the death of Jesus marked not an end and a defeat but a victory and a new beginning.

Those who are touched by and believe in Peter's message

are baptized in the name of Jesus. They give themselves over in faith to him and seek from him the forgiveness of their sins. Through baptism they receive the gift of the Spirit, the Spirit of the risen Christ, the Spirit without whose presence they will be unable to live as true disciples of Jesus.

The second reading evokes the extraordinary patience and endurance of Jesus in the face of suffering. What made his attitude all the more striking was his innocence. In all that he underwent he entrusted himself to God. By doing so, he won for us forgiveness; "By his wounds [we] have been healed."

Guardian of Our Souls

The passage goes on to describe the risen Christ as the shepherd and guardian of our souls. The language is similar to that of the gospel. In all that Jesus said and did he revealed a deep compassion and concern for people. He cared in a special way for the poor and sinners, for those who were sick or disabled or who for other reasons were pushed to the margins of society.

The Easter faith affirms that what Jesus did during his earthly life he continues to do for us. He does it directly and mysteriously through the gift of the Spirit active in the recesses of our hearts. He does it indirectly through word and sacrament and the structured life of the community of faith and through the encouragement that we give to one another.

The Greek word here for "guardian" is the same word that is translated elsewhere as "bishop." Later, Peter describes the responsibility of Christian leaders as that of shepherding. Ordained and non-ordained ministers alike are called in their pastoral ministry to embody and give human form to the care and concern of the eternal shepherd.

Abundant Life

Today's gospel ends with a striking expression of the meaning of Jesus' life and destiny. He came that we might have life and have it in abundance. The theme of life is central to John's portrayal of Jesus. He is the bread of life, living water, the vine in whom we are called to live, the source of eternal life. The life that Jesus offers is above all life from God, life that perfects this life and brings it to fulfillment.

Our God is a God of life. He is the creator God from whom all life comes and on whom it depends. In spite of sin and self-destructiveness, God did not withdraw his gift of life but sent Jesus to renew it. The resurrection of Jesus proclaims the triumph of life, a triumph that he experienced in his own being, but a triumph that is also meant to be shared in by us.

To believe in the risen Christ and to open ourselves to his gifts is to place ourselves and all that we do in the service of life. We are called to be instruments of Christ's life-giving, life-enhancing care and concern for the world and for humankind.

A Royal Priesthood

5TH SUNDAY OF EASTER
Readings: Acts 6:1-7, 1 Pet 2:4-9, Jn 14:1-12

Today's gospel is from John's account of Jesus' discourse after the last supper. He encourages the disciples to take heart and to believe both in him and in God. Although they are troubled and saddened at his talk about leaving them, he assures them that his departure is for their benefit. He is going to the Father in order to prepare a place for them, but before long he will return and take them with him.

In spite of the clarity with which Jesus formulates his promise, the disciples fail to understand. And so he sums up the meaning of his life and mission with the phrase: "I am the way and the truth and the life." In Jesus, God has both revealed himself to us and offered us a share in his life. Jesus and the Father are so much one that to see Jesus is to see the Father.

The death and resurrection of Jesus opened up a new moment in the story of salvation. Initially believers thought that it would be a brief one. They hoped that Jesus would soon return and usher in God's kingdom in its definitive state. In fact, however, the moment turned into decades and centuries and even millennia. It became the time of the church.

Built into a Spiritual House

Today's second reading from 1 Peter contains an inspiring vision of what it means to be church. Jesus, the risen Lord, is, of course, at the heart of Christian life. To be baptized is to be enabled to share his life and to take on something of his dignity. It is also to become a member of a special community.

The text weaves together a series of biblical images in order to form a new pattern. Although despised and rejected by human beings, Jesus, in God's eyes, is chosen and precious. He is a living stone, the cornerstone, on which God intends to build a new and spiritual temple. Rooted in Christ, we are living stones being built up with and by him into a spiritual house, a community of faith, in which God can dwell.

Jesus was not a priest in any ordinary sense of the word. He was not, for example, of the tribe of Levi nor did he officiate, as priests did, at the sacrificial ritual in the temple at Jerusalem. If, in spite of that, early Christianity proclaimed him the perfect priest, it was because it interpreted his whole life and especially the self-giving love that led to his death as a supreme act of sacrifice and worship.

Spiritual Sacrifices

To be baptized in Jesus is, among other things, to be baptized into his priesthood. All of us together form what Peter describes as "a holy priesthood" called to offer "spiritual sacrifices" to God through Christ. Striking here is the emphasis on the corporate nature of our priesthood. We are not priests in isolation, but precisely as members of Christ's body.

The idea of "spiritual sacrifices" suggests the role that the Spirit plays in the Christian life. Through the Spirit we are united with Jesus and thus enabled to live the kind of life he lived, the life that constitutes the authentic sacrifice.

The sacrifice to which we are called is above all the sacrifice of life. If it involves prayer and worship, it also includes love and service. All of this comes together in a special way in the eucharist. There the sacrifice of Jesus is rendered present so that we may be transformed by it.

Choosing the Seven

The reading from Acts also talks about the time of the church. It is remarkable in the honesty with which it reflects the tensions that threatened community life from the beginning. It is also instructive and hopeful in what it has to say about the creativity of the apostles in responding to new needs.

Greek-speaking members of the community complain that their social needs are not being dealt with fairly. The twelve apostles recognize the problem but find themselves unable on their own to meet it. They invite the Hellenists to choose seven men from among themselves capable of taking on the responsibility. The result is the beginning of local ministry.

The time of the church is not always an easy one. It falls between the life of the earthly Jesus and the moment of final fulfillment. It is a time that is sometimes marked by tension and conflict and that periodically throws up new and difficult challenges that demand from both leaders and people creative and courageous decisions. The time of the church, however, is also the time of the Spirit. It is he who inspires and strengthens us in our efforts to be a community of faith.

Spirit of Truth

6TH SUNDAY OF EASTER
Readings: Acts 8:5-8, 14-17, 1 Pet 3:15-18, Jn 14:15-21

Today's gospel is taken once again from John's account of the discourse of Jesus after the last supper. The new theme that it introduces is that of the Paraclete, a word that can be translated as advocate or counselor or helper. If Jesus' death will mark the end of his physical presence among the disciples, he has no intention of leaving them orphans. In answer to his prayer the Father will give them "another Paraclete."

The use of the word "another" here suggests how closely the relationship between Jesus and the one he promises to send has to be understood. The Paraclete will carry forward Jesus' role and activity. Put perhaps more precisely, the risen Christ himself will continue to be active among his followers in and through the gift of the Spirit.

Jesus identifies the Paraclete as "the Spirit of truth," that is, as the Spirit who will lead the disciples into the truth. The truth to which Jesus seems to be referring is primarily the truth about himself and his relation to the Father and about the divine indwelling of Father, Son and Spirit that he is offering to those who believe in him.

The Need for Love

Jesus invites us to love him and affirms that if we do the Father will love us and will come with Jesus to live in us. However precisely this is understood, it cannot mean that our love is the condition for God's love. The emphasis of John's whole gospel is exactly the opposite. It is God who first loves us. And yet our love is not without its significance.

For John the final meaning of life and indeed of all reality is summed up in the phrase "God is love." Motivated only by love,

God sent his Son to reveal himself to us and to share with us his life. Through the Spirit present in our hearts we are brought alive in Christ. We come to know as it were from within the intimacy that exists between Jesus and the Father. We know it and are invited to share in it.

To love Jesus means to keep his commandments, to follow his example, to walk the way that he walked. If there is one word in John's gospel that sums up Jesus' life and teaching, it is again love. We are to love one another as he loved us. Such love is both the fruit of, and the condition for, God's presence in us.

Sanctify Christ Our Lord

The background for today's second reading is suffering and persecution. In the face of life's inevitable difficulties Peter encourages his readers and us to be patient and steadfast and above all to focus on the example of Jesus. In a striking phrase he invites us to sanctify Christ in our hearts, to cherish him as the norm and pattern of our lives, to let his presence expand and grow and fill our minds and imaginations.

Jesus, as Peter puts it, died in order to bring us to God. The phrase is reminiscent of our gospel reading. Christianity is not primarily about rules and regulations, rituals and institutions. It has to do above all with the presence in us of the God of self-communicating love.

We are brought to God by spiritual transformation. It is the Spirit who draws us into relationship with Jesus and who in and through him opens us in a new way to the mystery of God present in the depths of our being. In Jesus we are alive not only with the natural life that animates our bodies and minds and hearts, but with the very life of God.

Jesus and the Spirit

As an historical person who lived some two thousand years ago Jesus remains a remarkable teacher and a wonderful example of the religious and moral life. For believers, however, he is more than that. As our second reading formulates it, he was put to death in the flesh but made alive in the spirit. In the gospel Jesus says: "Because I live, you also will live."

Today's first reading tells about the spread of the Christian message from Jerusalem to Samaria. Philip and others preached the good news about Jesus, and many were baptized in his name. It was only, however, when Peter and John came and laid hands on them that they received the Spirit.

Once the gift of the Spirit has sealed our unity with Christ, his words and example take on new meaning. They come alive in our hearts and inspire us to be like him. This is what Paul means when he says that he has put on Christ and that for him to live is Christ. It is the Holy Spirit, the Paraclete, who transforms us into the likeness of Jesus.

Above Every Name

ASCENSION OF THE LORD
Readings: Acts 1:1-11, Eph 1:17-23, Mt 28:16-20

The ascension is an integral moment in the unfolding of the paschal mystery. Far from being a return to this life, the resurrection of Jesus was a breakthrough, as it were, to final and definitive life. The Easter season and all its parts proclaim that Jesus lives, that he lives with God and that he lives for us. What is characteristic for Luke of the ascension is that it marks the end of a period of appearances of the risen Jesus and the beginning of a new mode of his presence to us.

Today's second reading speaks in highly imaginative terms of the exaltation of Christ, of his being seated at the right hand of God. He is established above every power and dominion and authority, in fact above every created reality. The ascension affirms that the humanity of Jesus has been taken up into the mystery of God and has become the key and focal point for the whole of creation. The risen Christ shares in the lordship of God. He is the head of all creation and in a special way of the church which is his body.

Promise of the Spirit

The ascension is the necessary pre-condition for the coming of the Spirit. Even as Jesus leaves his disciples, he tells them that in a way analogous to the baptism of John they will be plunged into, and gifted with, the Holy Spirit. He will come upon them and fill them with strength and courage and enable them to become witnesses of all that Jesus did and taught.

The disciples still do not understand everything that has happened and its meaning for them and for the world. They ask Jesus whether he will now restore the kingdom to Israel. Instead of being given an answer, they are told that it is not for them to know the times and seasons of God's saving activity.

What Jesus offers is not knowledge about how our life and human history will unfold but rather the promise of the healing and renewing presence among us of the Holy Spirit. The disciples are assured that Jesus will one day return in glory. Until that day, life will go on, but for them it will be different because Christ's Spirit will be with them.

Be My Witnesses

The resurrection and ascension mark the end of one moment in the story of salvation and the beginning of another. In the life, teaching, and destiny of Jesus, God both revealed his plan for us and brought about a renewal of our lives. What was begun then has to continue, and it has to continue not only in the depths of individual hearts but in an explicit and visible way as well. It has to continue in a living community of disciples.

The New Testament word for church, *ekklesia*, means a coming together of people in response to a call — in this instance, in response to the preaching of the gospel. Called into being by the Easter message and by the story of Jesus, the Christian community exists to keep alive his memory and to bear witness before the world to all that he said and did.

In today's gospel the risen Christ appears to the eleven and charges them with the task of making disciples of all nations. They are to teach what Jesus taught and baptize people in the name of the triune God. As they attempt to fulfill this mission he promises to be with them until the end of time.

A Spirit of Wisdom

Today's second reading begins with a prayer. Paul asks God to fill us with a spirit of wisdom and understanding so that we may know the power of God and gain some insight into the riches and the glory of the inheritance to which he has called us. What God has done in the resurrection and exaltation of Jesus is a promise of what he will do for us.

The Easter faith has as much to say about God as about Jesus. It reveals him as a living God, a God of the living, a God of life and not of death. He is on our side as we struggle to live, to live fully and authentically, to live as God wants us to live. God's power for life is poured out on us in the form of the Spirit. It is present in us as individuals but also as members of the community of faith.

To bear witness to Jesus and to what God has done for us in him is something that involves both word and deed. We need, of course, to tell the story of Jesus and to proclaim his teaching, but we need every bit as much to try to embody in our lives all that he stands for. Although this is beyond our natural capacity, it becomes possible through the power of the Spirit. It is the Spirit who molds us into the body of Christ.

Glorify Your Son

7TH SUNDAY OF EASTER
Readings: Acts 1:12-14, 1 Pet 4:13-16, Jn 17:1-11a

Today's gospel contains part of the prayer that brings to a climax John's account of Jesus' discourse at the last supper. It begins, as the "Our Father" begins, with a direct and simple address to the one Jesus called Father. What it asks first is that the Father glorify his Son so that the Son may glorify him.

Although present throughout the New Testament the theme of glory is particularly central in John. Its Hebrew equivalent *kabod* was used in the Jewish tradition in relation to visible manifestations of God's power. It was something that God revealed in his saving activity and on occasion in the splendor of temple worship. Beyond power and majesty the term evokes radiance and beauty. Although belonging by its nature to God, divine glory can and sometimes is shared with people.

As the prayer begins Jesus announces that his hour has come, a phrase that refers to his passion, death and resurrection. Together they constitute Jesus' return to the Father, his entry into God's glory. The prayer makes clear that the process of his passover from this world to the next involves at each stage the glorification both of the Father and of Jesus.

To Give Eternal Life

If the word glory primarily points to something that belongs to God and that can be shared in by Jesus and to a different degree by us, it also refers to the praise and honor that we give God in recognition of his glory. When Jesus says that he glorified God on earth, he probably means that in and through his activity God's glory became visible. He may also mean that his life and teaching were of such a kind as to lead people to give praise and glory to God for what God was doing through them.

Jesus glorified God by fulfilling his will. In the present passage he indicates what this entailed by saying that he was sent to bring eternal life to those whom God would entrust to him. Eternal life involves a knowing of the true God and of Jesus Christ. This is something that is more than simply intellectual. It is inseparable from love and commitment. Unlike the other evangelists John rarely refers to the kingdom of God. For him Jesus' mission is above all to make known God's name, to communicate God's word and to call people to faith.

Sharing Christ's Sufferings

Jesus goes on to pray for the disciples. If he is on the point of leaving this world for the next, they must remain where they are. In spite of the Paraclete which he has already promised to send them, he knows that their situation will not always be easy. The world will reject them as it has rejected him. He prays that God will be with them and strengthen them.

Today's second reading is from the first letter of Peter. Written at a time when the early Christian community was faced with the threat of persecution, it reminds its readers and us of the possible positive meaning that suffering and persecution can have. Through them we can share in the sufferings of Christ.

Like John, Peter too has recourse to the language of glory. To be abused because of Christ, he says, is to receive "the spirit of glory, which is the Spirit of God." With us as with Jesus the path of suffering leads to resurrection and to a share in the glory of God. For this reason we ought to give glory and praise to God even in the midst of pain and struggle.

Waiting in Prayer

In his last supper discourse Jesus sometimes speaks as if he has already entered into glory. His words seem to take on a transhistorical quality. They are addressed to believers of every age as much as to the first disciples.

The time between ascension and Pentecost is a time of watching and waiting. Our first reading recounts how the apostles returned to Jerusalem after Jesus had ascended and how together with Mary and the other women they gathered in the upper room and waited in prayer for the coming of the Spirit that Jesus had promised.

The glorification of Jesus through his death and resurrection was not meant for him alone. It had saving value that was to bear fruit in the lives of believers throughout history. The way this was to happen was through the coming of the Spirit. Today's liturgy reminds us of our need to enter into the attitude of the disciples waiting for the first Pentecost. We need to turn in trusting prayer to God and to open ourselves to his gift. Only by the power of the Spirit can we truly be people of faith.

Spirit of Christ

PENTECOST SUNDAY
Readings: Acts 2:1-11, 1 Cor 12:3b-7, 12-13, Jn 20:19-23

Pentecost makes explicit one of the central aspects of the Easter mystery. Through the resurrection Jesus has entered into a new relationship not only with God but also with us. As the risen Christ he continues to inspire and guide us and to be the one with and in whom we worship and praise God. He does all these things, however, through the power of the Spirit. For Christians the Spirit is no longer simply the Spirit of God, he is also and inseparably the Spirit of the risen Christ.

The Pentecost story evokes the forces of nature to suggest the power and the vitality of the Spirit. His coming is like a rush of wind and his presence like tongues of fire. The immediate result of the Spirit's descent is a revelation of the universality of the apostolic mission. The message of salvation is to be preached to people of every nation and culture. The obvious reference to the story of Babel suggests that the gospel is to heal divided humanity not by eliminating its many languages but by preaching in them a unifying message of peace and reconciliation. The miracle of Pentecost reveals the Spirit as the ground and inspiration of the church's catholicity.

Peace and Forgiveness

In today's gospel the risen Christ twice greets the disciples with the phrase: "Peace be with you." The repetition suggests that more than a casual greeting is meant. Shalom or peace is something that we long and work for and that finally we hope for from God. Beyond the absence of violence and conflict, it implies harmony and justice and the fullness of life.

Because of the life and destiny of Jesus, God's peace is

111

among us in a new way. Paul explained it in terms of reconciliation. In Christ God reconciled us to himself and to one another. A
power for reconciliation has been let loose in the world; it is
meant to touch and transform individuals and peoples.

Jesus commissions the disciples to continue his mission, and
to help them he breathes on them the gift of the Spirit. They are to
make God's forgiveness available through the preaching of the
gospel and through baptism. The church is to be a reconciled and
reconciling community, all aspects of whose life, including the
sacrament of reconciliation, are to bear witness to and to mediate
God's forgiveness.

To Drink of the Spirit

For Paul the Spirit is an inner principle of Christian life.
Today's second reading underlines how a living relationship to
Christ is only possible through the Spirit. Without the Spirit, there
is no real faith in Jesus. The Spirit binds us to Christ and in Christ
to one another, thus forming his body.

The Spirit is a source of variety as well as of unity. Paul insists that all Christians receive from the Spirit gifts that are to be
put to the service of the common good. Education, wealth, social
standing, even ecclesial office are secondary. What makes us
Christians and enables us to contribute to our life together is the
presence in us of the Spirit and of his gifts.

With his mention of the Spirit, the Lord, and God, Paul
evokes the mystery of the Trinity. Salvation, as creation, begins
with the Father but is carried out by Christ in the power of the
Spirit. Our response to God, on the other hand, is effected by the
Spirit who unites us with Christ through and with whom we
praise and worship God and give him glory.

Life and Renewal

The biblical word for Spirit means wind and breath and, by
implication, principle of life. The Spirit is a Spirit of life and is
associated with both creation and the new creation in Christ. The

Spirit suggests something dynamic and alive, something that moves and inspires, that illumines and transforms.

When, as Christians, we speak of spirituality or of the spiritual life, what we mean more than anything else is the presence and activity of the Spirit of Christ in us, molding us into Christ's likeness. Through the Spirit we put on Christ, are gradually healed and renewed from within, so that finally we can say with Paul: "I live now not I but Christ lives in me."

What is true of us as individuals is also true of us as a community of faith. The Spirit is the life principle of the church. With Vatican II John XXIII hoped for a new Pentecost, a new springtime for the church. We are far from exhausting its potential for renewal. Now as always we need the Spirit to enlighten our minds, spark our imaginations and fill our hearts with his life-giving love.

Trinity Sunday and Corpus Christi

God Is Love

TRINITY SUNDAY
Readings: Ex 34:4b-6, 8-9, 2 Cor 13:11-13, Jn 3:16-18

The Christian experience and understanding of God is rooted in what seems like a profound paradox. Like Judaism before it, Christianity proclaims a radical monotheism. The Lord our God is one. He is both creator and redeemer. Within God's oneness, however, we have come to discern a fullness of life that we invoke with the names Father, Son and Spirit.

The doctrine of the Trinity is not a puzzle or a conundrum but rather an attempt to point believers to the mystery of the inner life of God such as it has been revealed to us in the story of salvation. Our sense of God is inseparable from the life and destiny of Jesus and from our experience of the Spirit of God and of the risen Christ alive and active among us.

The liturgy, as so much of Christian life, presupposes and reinforces an awareness of God as a trinitarian mystery. The eucharistic prayer, to take the most obvious example, is directed to the Father, in and through the Son, in the unity of the Holy Spirit. We pray to God to send the Spirit on the bread and wine and on us that they and we might be transformed into Christ.

Merciful and Gracious

Today's first reading evokes the story of the covenant. For the Israelites God was in a special way their God, the one who in mercy and love had responded to them in their need and rescued them out of slavery. He brought them out of Egypt in order to seal a covenant, to establish a permanent relationship, with them. He would be their God and they would be his people.

Moses is the instrument of God's saving presence in the midst of Israel. Through him the commandments are given and the covenant is sealed. In our reading, God reveals the qualities that are his as the God of the covenant. He is neither distant nor indifferent but full of mercy and tenderness. He cares about human beings and wants to be with them.

In making the covenant God commits himself to Israel and through Israel to the whole of humanity. His commitment is definitive; it will never be withdrawn. No matter how faithless and indifferent our response, God's attitude will be marked by "steadfast love and faithfulness." In the face of our inadequacies and sinfulness, God remains "slow to anger," rich in mercy.

He Sent His Son

The coming of Jesus does not contradict but rather deepens Israel's experience of God. Their God, the nearness of whose kingdom Jesus proclaims, is the God of creation and of covenant, the God of human fulfillment. Today's gospel reading takes us to the heart of John's understanding both of the person of Jesus and of what his life and destiny reveal of God.

Jesus, like Moses and the prophets, is an instrument of God's saving activity. He is like them but at the same time more than them. He is the perfect servant of God who both proclaims and is God's word. He is the incarnation of divine wisdom and of divine love and mercy. Jesus is, in a unique way, God's Son.

The life and destiny of Jesus are inseparable from the Spirit. It is by the power of the Spirit that Jesus fulfills his ministry and that he continues to be active among us. To think of God's love for us is to think also and inevitably of Jesus and of the transforming presence of his Spirit among us.

The Communion of the Holy Spirit

Today's second reading contains the closing verses of Paul's second letter to the church at Corinth. In writing it Paul has been both angry and severe about some of the divisions and abuses that had grown up among the members of that community. He ends with an appeal for harmony and order and prays that the God of love and peace will be with them.

His final greeting suggests how early Christian experience was pushing people to think of God's relation to them in a trinitarian way. Everything begins with the love of God. It is because God is love and because God loves us that he sent Jesus to effect our salvation. What God has done for us through him is pure grace. It establishes us in an intimate relationship of communion with the Holy Spirit.

The God revealed to us in Jesus Christ is a God of infinite love. If God's love is manifested outside of God for the first time in creation, its original form is that of the inner divine life in which from all eternity Father, Son and Spirit have rejoiced in an unending reciprocal love. Christian life here and now is a sharing in this love through the communion of the Spirit. It will be brought to fulfillment in eternal life.

Table of the Lord

SOLEMNITY OF THE BODY AND BLOOD OF CHRIST
Readings: Deut 8:2-3, 14b-16, 1 Cor 10:16-17, Jn 6:51-59

The eucharist is a rich and many-sided reality that stands at the heart of our lives both as individuals and as the church. In it we praise and thank God for his gifts and especially for the gift of Jesus Christ. We repeat the words over the bread and the wine that Jesus spoke at the last supper and in doing so we make memory of him and his life and render present among us the power for forgiveness and renewal of his death and resurrection.

In identifying the bread as his body, his person, given and broken for us, and the wine as his life blood poured out for the forgiveness of sins, Jesus revealed the nature of the extraordinary gift that he was leaving to us. Salvation, reconciliation and eternal life are inseparable from him. Jesus not only brings God's gift to us, he is that gift in person.

The obvious meaning of the choice by Jesus of bread and wine as symbols for the sacrament of his presence among us is that he wants to give himself to us as food for our journey. In the eucharist the risen Christ continues to be present, inviting us to his table and offering us a share in his life.

Living Bread

Although the gospel of John does not include in its account of the last supper any reference to the words that Jesus said over the bread and the wine, it does refer explicitly to the eucharist in its chapter 6, in Jesus' sermon on the bread of life. The first part of the sermon identifies Jesus as someone who has come from God, someone in whom divine wisdom dwells. Those who turn to him in faith are promised eternal life.

The last part of the sermon, which constitutes today's gospel reading, focuses on the eucharist. Jesus offers himself in the sacramental bread and wine as spiritual food and drink. He is the living bread, the bread that is both alive and gives life. The life he gives can be experienced here and now, but it will only be brought to fulfillment in eternity.

Through the eucharist, Jesus says, we are able to abide in him and he in us. Just as he has come from the Father and lives because of him, so will we live because of Jesus. The eucharist is more than a source of faith and courage. It is the living presence among us of the risen Christ. To share in it is to share in the most intimate way imaginable in his life.

One Bread, One Body

Our reading from 1 Corinthians makes the same point as the gospel. In the eucharist we participate in, have communion with, the body and blood of Christ. In doing so, we become one with him. It is for this reason, Paul says, that believers are to have nothing to do with whatever is at odds with Christ.

There is nothing magical about the eucharist. It focuses and renders concrete and accessible the offer of Christ's love and life. We must both approach it in faith and try to lead a life that corresponds to all that it implies. Paul does not hesitate to tell those who in gathering for the eucharist despise and disregard the poor among them that it is not truly the Lord's supper that they celebrate.

Our relation to Christ in the eucharist has implications for our relationship to others. By partaking of the one bread, we who are many become one body, the body of Christ. In drawing closer to Christ we cannot help but draw closer to one another. It is impossible to love and respect the eucharistic Christ without having love and respect for all who constitute his body.

Church and Eucharist

The eucharist is at the center of what it is to be church. As a community of faith, the church is rooted in the life, teaching and destiny of Jesus. It lives in him and in virtue of the saving power of his death and resurrection. God has called the church into existence in order to keep alive the memory of Jesus and to announce his offer of salvation to all peoples.

In celebrating the eucharist the church celebrates and renews the mystery of its own inner life and bears witness to it before the world. The self-giving love of Jesus present in the eucharist both nourishes the church and challenges it to become in all that it does a sacrament of Christ's presence.

It is at the table of the Lord that in a special way the church receives the nourishment and strength it needs to carry out its mission. As with Israel in the desert, God is ever among us, sustaining us with his gifts. In the eucharist, the risen Christ continues, through the Spirit, to be with us and to be for us a promise of eternal fulfillment.

Ordinary Time: Sundays 9 to 34

Founded on Rock

9TH SUNDAY IN ORDINARY TIME
Readings: Deut 10:12-13a; 11:18, 26-28, 32,
Rom 1:16-17; 3:20-26, 28, Mt 7:21-27

Today's gospel contains the concluding section of the sermon on the mount. In it Jesus underlines in the clearest possible fashion the radical significance for us of his moral teaching. Good and loving action and not simply religious phrases and practices will be the focus of our future judgment. Those whom Jesus on that day will recognize as his own are those who will have struggled to put his teaching into practice.

The image of the house for the self is very ancient. As used in the present context by Jesus it evokes the inevitable trials and sufferings of life. Those who both hear and act on his teaching, Jesus suggests, have a place to stand. Like everyone else they are exposed to storm and wind, but because they are founded on the rock of real commitment, they will not fall. Jesus calls those who fail to respond to his invitation "foolish." Lacking roots and any real sense of moral identity, they will be overcome by the challenges of life and will eventually suffer religious and human collapse. The image of the two houses, the one built on rock and the other on sand, is as evocative today as it was in Jesus' time.

The Need To Choose

Earlier in the sermon on the mount, Jesus affirmed that he had come not to abolish the law or the prophets, but rather to fulfill them. In what sense this might be understood is suggested by today's first reading. It reveals a parallel between the conditions for the covenant made by God through Moses with Israel and the teaching of Jesus.

The word "covenant," meaning an agreement or contract,

was used by biblical writers to express their understanding of God's relationship to Israel. In the exodus God revealed himself as a God of liberation and salvation. He intervened on behalf of Israel and in doing so declared his desire to make of them his special people. The covenant, however, required two partners. God's love and action called for a human response.

In today's reading Moses challenges the people to choose and to commit themselves to the covenant. They are to love God with all their heart and soul and to walk in God's ways. If they do so they will be blessed; if not, they will be abandoned to their lot. The parallel with the gospel is striking.

Justification by Faith

At first glance the message of today's second reading, taken from Paul's letter to the Romans, seems different from, if not at odds with, the other two readings. Paul insists that we are not justified or made righteous by fulfilling the works of the law. In fact, according to Paul, such fulfillment is impossible. In terms of the law we are all sinners.

The first two verses of the reading sum up forcefully Paul's deepest conviction about the meaning of the gospel. In the good news of and about Jesus Christ, God's saving power has been revealed in the midst of human life. Through the death and resurrection of Jesus God offers salvation and new life to everyone. In order to receive them, we must turn to God in faith and in utter trust. Recognizing our own incapacity to live a life of genuine goodness, we need to open ourselves to the gift of God's healing Spirit.

Faith and Action

If Paul focuses on the great event of God's saving action in Jesus and especially on his death and resurrection, he knows that faith must become operative through love. It has to make a difference in the way we live. The Spirit we receive is a Spirit of peace and joy, of goodness and love, a Spirit who enables us to put on Christ and to walk in his ways.

At first view, the sermon on the mount seems to offer an impossible ideal. Who can be as generous and loving and self-forgetful as it implies? It is beyond anything that we can do on our own. What makes it possible is the gift of God.

Jesus began his public life by preaching the in-breaking of the kingdom or reign of God. What he meant above all by this was God's healing and forgiving presence among us. Jesus called people to faith in his message and to conversion of life. The sermon on the mount spells out the kind of attitudes and actions he expected from those who would commit themselves to become his disciples. Paul's teaching on justification by faith emphasizes our need for renewal and healing. With Christ's Spirit in our hearts, however, Paul was convinced that we can live the gospel. It remains now as always both gift and challenge.

Mercy, Not Sacrifice

10TH SUNDAY IN ORDINARY TIME
Readings: Hos 6:3-6, Rom 4:18-25, Mt 9:9-13

All the gospels bear witness that some of the most knowledgable and committed religious people among Jesus' contemporaries were scandalized at many of the things that he did. This is the case once again in today's reading. A group of Pharisees are baffled that Jesus insists on eating with those whose whole way of life condemns them to live on the margin of respectable society. What makes Jesus' action so provocative is that in eating with social outcasts and sinners he seems to suggest that his message and mission are directed in a special way to them.

In responding to criticism, Jesus affirms that this is indeed the case. It is primarily for such people that he has come. His gift is not power or privilege but healing and forgiveness. Only those who know their need for such things are able to welcome him. Those, on the other hand, who are scandalized at his generosity seem to have fallen into the trap of self-righteousness. To them Jesus cites an oracle of the prophet Hosea: "I desire mercy, not sacrifice." The phrase, in the present context, means that a compassionate outreach to sinners outweighs any legalistic insistence on the letter of the law.

Love and Knowledge

Today's first reading contains in a slightly different form the text to which Jesus referred. It is part of a larger judgment proclaimed by the prophet against his contemporaries. They had abandoned the covenant and had begun worshiping other gods. Through the prophet the Lord confronts them with their infidelity: "Your love is like the morning cloud, like the dew that goes away early." What he desires of them is *hesed*, or steadfast love, and the knowledge of God.

The Hebrew word *hesed* stands at the center of the biblical understanding of the relationship between God and Israel. Everything that God did for the people revealed him as a God of love and mercy. In the covenant he promised that his love would be everlasting. What he asked in return was loving fidelity.

The knowledge that God desires is in no sense abstract or technical. It is a knowledge that comes from experience and commitment. Hosea compares it to the knowledge that grows out of a faithful and intimate relationship between husband and wife.

Healer and Physician

In spite of its brevity and simplicity, today's gospel story throws considerable light on the way that Jesus understood both himself and his ministry. He comes from God; he comes not to bring judgment and condemnation but mercy and healing. As the deeply religious person that he is, Jesus' whole being is focused on God. This tends to relativize everything else. He knows the meaning, and respects the value, of the religious laws and traditions of his people but he refuses to allow them to impede in any way God's present and overflowing mercy.

Forms and practices, rituals and ways of life have an important function in our religious life. When they are used as they are meant to be used, they facilitate our encounter with God and help to open us to his gifts. The liturgy in particular is a privileged moment for experiencing and deepening our identity as the body of Christ. And yet such things, good in themselves, can become harmful if they are not approached with the right mind and heart. Today's gospel with its insistence on "mercy, not sacrifice" reminds us of this.

Trusting Faith

In the second reading Paul appeals to the figure of Abraham in order to express his conviction that we are justified or made righteous before God not by works, but by faith. The particular moment in Abraham's story on which he focuses is striking. From a human point of view there was little hope that the aged and barren couple would ever be able to have a child. "Hoping against hope," Abraham believed in God's promise and, because he did, he and Sarah became the parents of a great people. Their trusting faith made them just in God's sight.

Christians are called, Paul says, to an analogous attitude. In spite of our sinfulness and brokenness, God has taken the initiative and healed and forgiven us through the death and resurrection of Jesus. What is required of us is that we believe in what God has done and open ourselves to his gift.

For Paul as for Jesus the essence of religion is not to be found in rituals or laws but in an attitude of heart. Faith marks the beginning of the Christian life. It is meant to grow and to bear fruit in a life of love, justice and mercy.

Reconciled and Reconciling

11TH SUNDAY IN ORDINARY TIME
Readings: Ex 19:1-6a, Rom 5:6-11, Mt 9:36–10:8

Today's gospel underlines forcefully to what an extent Jesus' mission was focused on the people of Israel. As he looked around at his compatriots he was struck by how buffeted and abandoned they seemed. He thought of them as sheep without a shepherd. In order to bring to them more effectively his message of the nearness of God's kingdom he chose twelve from among his disciples and sent them out to neighboring towns and villages.

Although we often associate the number twelve with the apostles, the latter term seems to have had a broader application in the early church and in its more technical sense to have been tied up with the resurrection. The number twelve by itself, on the other hand, had a special meaning within the public life of Jesus. It called to mind the twelve tribes of Israel, each of which traced back its identity to one of the twelve sons of Jacob. Although the twelve tribes had long ceased to exist as identifiable units, it was hoped that their re-establishment would be part of the final coming of God's kingdom. The choosing by Jesus of twelve disciples to share in his ministry was a parable in action proclaiming that the kingdom was indeed at hand.

A Priestly Kingdom

Today's first reading evokes a particularly solemn moment in the history of Israel. Having escaped from Egypt, the people have come to Sinai where through Moses God invites them to enter into a covenant with him. In the chapters following our text the conditions of the covenant will be spelled out in terms of the code of law or Torah that is to govern their lives.

The present passage functions as an introduction to the

whole section. The Lord recalls how he liberated the people from among the Egyptians. "I bore you on eagles' wings and brought you to myself." The final phrase is revealing. Everything that God has done has had a particular goal in view. He intervened on their behalf so that they might become his people, his special possession. They are to bear witness to him and to his saving purpose in the midst of the world. If the people embrace the covenant and commit themselves to a life according to it, God will make of them "a priestly kingdom and a holy nation."

Christ Died for Us

There are striking parallels between Moses and Jesus. Both proclaim God's offer of salvation to their contemporaries. Both spell out the kind of moral life involved in being God's people. It is probable that in bringing so much of the ethical teaching of Jesus together in the sermon on the mount, Matthew intended to draw a parallel between Jesus' teaching and the role of Moses in the promulgation of the Torah at Sinai.

Where Jesus and Moses differ dramatically is in the way that early Christianity made Jesus' death and resurrection the center of its faith. For the first Christians, Jesus was more than a prophet and teacher. The key to his life and identity was his death and resurrection in and through which they believed God was at work bringing about forgiveness and justification.

In the second reading Paul speaks of the saving act of God in Christ in terms of reconciliation. The slavery in which humanity finds itself is primarily spiritual. We tend to be trapped in sin and selfishness. These alienate us from God and one another and set us at odds with the rest of creation. In Christ that alienation, at least in principle, has been overcome.

A Community of Reconciliation

If the mission of the twelve had a particular meaning in the life of Jesus, for the first readers of Matthew's gospel as well as for us it has additional implications. The twelve point ahead to the church and to its task of continuing in time and space the mission and ministry of Jesus.

The Christian life begins not with us but with God's saving and healing act in Christ. As Paul puts it, we have received reconciliation. This is the basis of our trust and of our hope. The love of God revealed in Christ knows no bounds. It is the rock upon which our individual and collective faith is grounded. Salvation comes from God and it comes as pure gift. But the gift is meant to bear fruit. Having ourselves been reconciled we are in turn invited to become instruments of reconciliation. No one can be a Christian simply for himself or herself. The church, called like Israel to be a priestly people, is to bear witness through word and action to the reconciling power let loose in the midst of human history through Christ and his Spirit. Like the twelve we are all to share in some way in the mission of Jesus.

Have No Fear

12TH SUNDAY IN ORDINARY TIME
Readings: Jer 20:7, 10-13, Rom 5:12-15, Mt 10:26-33

Today's first reading suggests something of the complex and deeply human response of Jeremiah to his prophetic vocation. The word of God initially entrusted to him was one of judgment and warning. He proclaims that if the people do not repent God will hand them over to their foes and that Jerusalem will be destroyed and its inhabitants driven into exile. Then as now, the bearer of such a message is exposed to ridicule and persecution.

Jeremiah's first reaction to what is happening is to inveigh against God. He accuses him of having enticed and seduced him, of having run roughshod over his hesitations and sense of inadequacy. Having proclaimed God's message, he has become a laughingstock, an object of scorn to the whole community.

If the prophet laments and complains, he remains a person of faith. He has committed himself to God and he trusts in God's fidelity. In the end, it is not his enemies who will triumph but Jeremiah or rather God whose word he has announced. In our text, as so often in the psalms, lamentation turns into praise and worship for the God who does not abandon his servants.

More Than Sparrows

The somewhat disparate sayings that constitute today's gospel are part of a larger set of instructions that Jesus gives to the twelve as they are sent out to proclaim the good news of the kingdom. In the section preceding our text, he warns them that they will encounter rejection and even hatred and persecution. He encourages them not to be afraid.

Although our passage was originally addressed to missionary preachers, its message applies to everyone. Faith is able to overcome fear precisely because it teaches us that those of whom in this life we might be afraid have no final power over us. God exists, and we belong to him. He is the only one whose judgment about us ultimately matters.

Although God's providence embraces the whole of creation and all its parts, it is exercised in a special way in regard to humanity. We are made in God's image and likeness and have been redeemed by Jesus Christ. We have received the gift of his Spirit and become his sisters and brothers. All these things taken together ground our unique dignity and value. They give us every reason for trust and hope.

Grace Abounds

One of the ways in which Paul tries to bring out the significance of Jesus for us and for the world is to compare him with Adam. The darker the picture he paints of humanity undermined by Adam's sin, the more dramatically the saving work of Christ stands out. Through Adam, Paul tells us in today's second reading, sin entered into the world and with sin death.

As the new Adam, Jesus marks the beginning of a new humanity. The image of God in which as children of Adam and Eve we share has been distorted by a long history of sin and self-destructiveness. Christ did not come to deny or destroy our humanity but rather to heal it and to help us become the kind of creatures that God intended us to be from the beginning.

Paul insists that the gift that is ours in Christ far outweighs the sinful state it was meant to overcome. As burdened as we continue to be by the effects of sin, we are to rejoice in God's grace revealed in Christ. His coming guarantees that in the end goodness and graciousness will triumph over all evil.

Acknowledged before God

The New Testament's emphasis on God's providence and on the superabounding nature of Christ's grace does not dispense us from our responsibility to respond to God's gifts and to cooperate with his will. Jesus puts it simply but forcefully in today's gospel reading. Those who acknowledge him before others, he will acknowledge before God; those who deny him, he will deny.

Historically the most dramatic form of acknowledgement of Jesus has been martyrdom. The very word means a witness. In the face of persecution and torture and even death people have borne witness to Christ and to the gospel. Their martyrdom has been a source of renewal and encouragement for the whole church.

Most of us will never be asked to undergo death for our faith. What we are invited to do is to live and die in ways that make evident that we are believers and that Christ's grace is indeed operative in us. Such things as honesty and loyalty, courage and goodness, willingness to put ourselves out for others and for what is right bear visible witness to our commitment to Christ. Such commitment will never be in vain.

Newness of Life

13TH SUNDAY IN ORDINARY TIME
Readings: 2 Kgs 4:8-12a, 14-17, Rom 6:3-4, 8-11, Mt 10:37-42

The sayings contained in today's gospel reading conclude the instructions given by Jesus to the twelve as he sends them out to preach the good news of the kingdom. Some of the sayings focus on the challenge involved in discipleship while others announce a reward for all who receive those whom Jesus has sent.

The presence of Jesus sometimes divides people by forcing them to make decisions. A serious attempt to embrace Christian discipleship, to live the vision of the gospel, can put one at odds not only with the values of the wider culture but also with the wishes and hopes of one's family and friends. Whoever, confronted with such a situation, opts for family is judged by Jesus as unfit to be his disciple.

The phrase about taking up one's cross and following Jesus comes back a number of times in the gospels. It takes on special meaning because of Jesus' own suffering and death. The fidelity that he brought to his mission knew no bounds. In one form or another the cross is a part of every life. What matters is that we recognize it and respond to it in the way that Jesus did.

To Lose One's Life

The ultimate challenge to the disciple is to be ready to give up or lose one's life for the sake of Jesus. Those who do so are promised that their death will lead to life. What is true of the end of life is also true of its midst. Those who are self-centered and seek only personal fulfillment and gratification will discover at the end that they are left with nothing.

Genuine fulfillment comes to those who are capable of self-forgetfulness, those who are able to go beyond the self and its preoccupations and give themselves to others, to life, and ultimately to God. The more we are concerned about ourselves the less chance we have of finding our true selves.

The paradox of life and death and of finding and losing one's self stands at the heart of Christian faith and experience. For Jesus, the way of rejection, suffering and death led to the triumph of the resurrection. By abandoning any hope of worldly success, he became for us a source of forgiveness and life.

Buried with Christ

The theme of death and life and of their interrelation is also central to our second reading. In baptism, Paul says, we are plunged into the death of Jesus; we are buried with him so that we can rise to newness of life. The death and resurrection of Jesus are more than a model that we are invited to imitate. In some way they touched and transformed the human situation, thus changing the deep meaning of our life and of human history.

Christianity offers more than an ethical ideal. It summons us through faith and through those symbolic rituals we call sacraments to enter into and share the life and destiny of Jesus. In Paul's view all that Jesus was and did come together and receive final meaning in his death and resurrection. To be baptized in Christ's death is to be brought into contact with his entire life. In baptism we die to self in order to come alive with the life of Christ. For Paul, complete sharing in the resurrection of Christ remains something that belongs to the future. In this life we continue to be exposed to sin and suffering and death. And yet through baptism something new has begun. We have died to sin and self-centeredness and are challenged to try to live for God and for one another.

The Reward of the Righteous

In the gospel Jesus affirms that those who welcome the preachers he sends welcome him and that those who welcome him welcome the God who sent him. To welcome Jesus is to open oneself to his message and to accept the gift of life and healing that he offers. It also implies a new way of life.

The reward that Jesus promises to those who accept him is ultimately eternal life with God. The first reading suggests that there can be a reward even in this life. The woman who welcomes Elisha as a holy man of God into her house is granted the desire of her heart. Equally striking are God's graciousness to her and the sensitivity of the prophet who appreciates what has been done for him and who understands the woman's longing.

The challenge of Jesus to take up the cross and to live a life of self-forgetfulness is beyond our own natural capacity. What alone makes it possible is the gift of the Spirit, a gift that we first receive in baptism and that touches and inspires us throughout the course of life. Through the Spirit, Christ lives in us, enabling us to walk in newness of life.

Come to Me

14TH SUNDAY IN ORDINARY TIME
Readings: Zech 9:9-10, Rom 8:9, 11-13, Mt 11:25-30

Today's gospel contains three separate but related sayings of Jesus, the third of which is well known and has been a source of consolation and encouragement for untold numbers of believers over the centuries. Jesus invites those who are tired and worn out by the challenges and burdens of life to come to him; with him they will find rest for their souls.

Whatever precise reference this saying had in the time of Jesus, it speaks today to people in a wide variety of situations. Our burden might be that of sickness or old age, family difficulties or financial problems. It might be the weight of years of responsibility in some profession or job. It might simply be the ongoing effort involved in trying to live a good and decent life.

Whatever our situation Jesus invites us to turn to him, to seek his help, to take on his yoke, his way of life. He describes himself in the language of the beatitudes. He is gentle and humble, welcoming and forgiving, ready to help those who come to him. The saying is an eloquent reminder of the centrality that Jesus is to have in our life and religion. Beyond doctrine and ritual and alone giving meaning to them is a concrete person offering acceptance and forgiveness, strength and rest.

Son of the Father

Jesus is able to offer us all that he does only because of his unique relationship to God. He identifies himself here as the Son to whom the Father has handed over all things. Much more than a loving and compassionate brother, a model of human goodness, Jesus is someone in whom and through whom God's graciousness has taken on a human face.

To come to Jesus presupposes that we believe in him, that we recognize his very special relationship to God and that we seek in him God's gift and love. As attractive and even mysterious as Jesus was both in his life and in his teaching, it is only when God, through the gift of the Spirit, actually reveals Jesus' true identity that we can recognize him for who and what he is.

Real faith in Jesus always involves an overcoming of the world, a going beyond of ordinary experience. Today's gospel begins with a prayer of Jesus in which he thanks the Father for having revealed his saving activity not to the wise and the intelligent but to infants, to those who in the eyes of the world are the little ones, the marginalized. It is only those who know their own limits and needs who are drawn to Jesus.

Spirit of Christ

Our reading from Paul evokes themes that are analogous to those in the gospel. He contrasts what he calls life in the flesh and life in the spirit. The flesh here is not the body in opposition to the soul but rather human life as cut off from God and turned in on itself. The spirit, on the other hand, points to human life as open to God and receptive to God's gifts.

We can only live spiritually if the Spirit of God dwells in us. God's Spirit is identified here with the Spirit of Christ. Having the Spirit, we belong to Christ, and because we do we are able to lead lives of faith and love.

Although invisible, the risen Jesus remains active in the world. The words he spoke in the course of his historical ministry inviting those he encountered to seek rest in him he now addresses to us. Through the word of the scriptures and the power of the Spirit he continues to be among us urging us to welcome his life-giving, life-sustaining presence into our lives.

My Yoke Is Easy

If Jesus invites us to find rest and strength in him, he also makes clear that coming to him involves what he calls embracing his yoke. The image that is used here is evocative of traditional

Jewish teaching about wisdom. It is a yoke that frees us from distractions, that focuses us and makes us pleasing to God. The wisdom Jesus teaches and embodies reveals something about God but also a great deal about what God wants from us.

As much as we naturally focus in today's reading on the gift that Jesus offers, it would be a distortion not to take seriously the demands that are implied in discipleship. Although Jesus describes his yoke as easy and his burden as light, the sermon on the mount makes clear that turning to him demands a way of life reflective of his own. The same teaching is to be found in Paul. Those who receive the gift of the Spirit are to live in ways that correspond to and reflect it. Whether we think of the Christian life in terms of imitating Jesus or of living according to his Spirit, our response to God's gift is an essential part of it.

Bearing Fruit

15TH SUNDAY IN ORDINARY TIME
Readings: Is 55:10-11, Rom 8:18-23, Mt 13:1-23

The story of the sower casting seed with seeming extravagance on fertile and infertile ground alike is well known. As in the case of so many of the parables it is open to a variety of interpretations. Within the context of Jesus' ministry it evokes his preaching of the nearness of the kingdom. Some do not listen to him at all; others do but refuse to allow themselves to be touched by what he says. Some, finally, hear and understand.

Although the parable mentions three different situations in which seeds fail to take root or develop, the emphasis is clearly on the extraordinary growth that does take place. Such astonishing fertility makes one forget the seed that bore no fruit. The parable is a promise that, in spite of apparent failure, the word of Jesus will one day bring forth a harvest beyond measure.

An analogous conviction about the power of God's word is reflected in our first reading. The text is from the end of that part of Isaiah known as the book of consolation. As surely as rain and snow water the earth, rendering it fertile, so God's word, once proclaimed, will fulfill his saving purpose.

Hearing and Understanding

In Matthew, the story of the sower becomes an occasion for reflecting on Jesus' use of parables. They are pointed stories that provoke attention and force people to think. Their very mysteriousness is part of their effectiveness. For those who refuse to listen, however, or who in listening are unable to understand, they become an impediment rather than a help.

The first Christians wondered why some responded in faith to Jesus while others did not. Freedom is obviously a factor but so is the saving will of God. No one comes to Jesus unless drawn by God. No one can listen to and understand Jesus' call if God's grace is not already operative in his or her heart. Only those eyes and ears which are blessed are able to see and hear.

In marked contrast to most parables, that of the sower is accompanied by an allegorical interpretation. Scholars disagree as to how precisely the original readers would have understood it. For Jewish Christians it might well have been related to the mystery of why they believed in Jesus while many of their compatriots did not. Others probably applied it to themselves and to their differing responses to the gospel.

The Groaning of Creation

The word of God sounds anew in every generation and in every life. It comes to us in a special way in the words of the scriptures, but it can also be heard in our heart and in our conscience. It relates to the issues and concerns that constitute what Vatican II has called the signs of the time.

Today's second reading is among the biblical texts cited by John Paul II in his various statements on the responsibility of individuals as well as states and international organizations to respond to the current ecological crisis. Paul relates the fate of creation to that of human beings. Our sinfulness has had destructive effects on the earth as well as on ourselves.

The first pages of Genesis affirm the radical goodness of the world as God's creation. They also reveal the special responsibility of humans, made in God's image, to be stewards of it. Paul sees creation and ourselves groaning and longing for final fulfillment. Even now we are called to do what we can to protect and foster life on earth.

Yielding Nothing

The gospel interpretation of the parable suggests some of the reasons why people fail to hear and respond to God's word. Sometimes the seed disappears almost as soon as it falls on the ground. Matthew speaks of the evil one snatching it away. Today we might think of the pace and noise and whirl of contemporary life which make it so difficult to be open to the spiritual.

Others have such a shallow interior life that even if the word penetrates their hearts, it disappears almost immediately. Finally, Jesus says, there are those who receive the word but are so caught up with "the cares of the world and the lure of wealth" that in the end God's word "yields nothing." The relevance of such an explanation in our culture is obvious.

The word of God calls us to faith and love, to hope and responsibility. It speaks to us about our personal life but also about our broader responsibilities. Whether we discern it in the scriptures or in the social teaching of the church or in the needs of others, it will bear fruit in us only to the degree that we welcome it into our hearts and commit ourselves to it.

Parables of Growth

16TH SUNDAY IN ORDINARY TIME
Readings: Wis 12:13, 16-19, Rom 8:26-27, Mt 13:24-43

Today's gospel contains three parables, each of which appeals to an ordinary and widely shared experience in order to throw some light on the kingdom of God or, as Matthew likes to call it, the kingdom of heaven. The stories reflect the world of Jesus and his first followers, a relatively simple world in which most people still lived close to the land.

The second and third parables emphasize the contrast between small beginnings and fairly substantial, even dramatic outcomes. A tiny seed is sown from which emerges eventually a scrub which then develops into a tree. A woman mixes a small amount of yeast with a batch of flour and produces a large number of loaves. The coming of God's kingdom is like such things.

In terms of world history nothing could have been more insignificant than the public ministry of Jesus. Without connections or money he appeared in a corner of the Roman empire proclaiming the nearness of God's reign and calling people to faith and conversion. Although his death seemed to dash whatever hopes he had awakened, it was not the end. By the resurrection Jesus' life and destiny became fruitful beyond expectation.

Good and Bad Seed

The first parable takes a different twist. The kingdom is again compared to someone sowing seed, only this time a second person comes along and sows weeds. In spite of a suggestion to pull up the weeds, the landowner decides to let the good and bad seed grow together. At harvest time a separation will be made.

The parable suggests a realism about life and a kind of tolerance. A concern for absolute purity and perfection can be destructive. On the other hand, and this is what is emphasized in the explanation contained in the second part of the reading, God will separate the good from the bad at the time of the final judgment. In this life it is not always possible to discern and to isolate what truly serves the kingdom.

The kingdom of which Jesus speaks is primarily God himself, God's presence, the reign of God's will in our lives. It depends radically upon God and God's initiative but it also comes in and through us. Most often it works its effect in the quiet and surprising way that a seed grows or that yeast leavens dough.

The Spirit Helps Us

We live in a world whose dominant values are rarely those preached by Jesus. The emphasis tends to be on success and getting ahead, on amassing material possessions and on being able to enjoy a certain style of life. It is striking how pervasive such things continue to be even in the face of economic difficulties and at a time when we are more aware than ever of how much so many around the world suffer under poverty and violence.

It is difficult in a world like ours to maintain a sense of what really matters and a commitment to it; it is even more difficult to communicate a conviction about such things to our children. Some are tempted to despair.

In today's second reading Paul proclaims a magnificent truth: "The Spirit helps us in our weakness." Although he is thinking primarily of our inability to pray as we would like, what he says applies to the whole of our moral and religious lives. Of ourselves, we are weak and fearful, but with God's Spirit active within us, we can bear real fruit.

With Sighs Too Deep for Words

Paul claims that we do not know how to pray as we ought. If that was true when he lived, it is even more true today. Part of the problem is that we are so distracted. Radio and television have become for many all but constant companions. It almost seems as if people are afraid to be alone, to be still, to listen to the pain and longings of their hearts.

Real prayer often uses fixed words but it is never just formulations. It rises up from our inner depths. As much as we try to worship and praise God, our most natural form of prayer in this life is the prayer of petition. We call out to God in our need and emptiness. We beg for mercy and strength and courage. The psalms are full of such prayers.

In a wonderful phrase Paul describes how the Spirit intercedes for us "with sighs too deep for words." Most often we do not recognize our true needs, our need for forgiveness and acceptance, for healing and love. We are too busy worrying about immediate concerns to think about ultimate ones. It is at that level that the Spirit prays within us. The God who searches and knows our hearts hears and answers the Spirit's prayer.

Hidden Treasure

17TH SUNDAY IN ORDINARY TIME
Readings: 1 Kgs 3:5-12, Rom 8:28-30, Mt 13:44-52

Today's gospel concludes the third of five major discourses or sermons that mark and give structure to Matthew's account of Jesus' life and teaching. This particular discourse contains seven or eight parables all of which in different ways touch on the varied responses, positive and negative, that people make to Jesus' preaching about the kingdom.

The parable of the net cast into the sea and brought to shore full of fish both good and bad is similar in its meaning to last week's parable about the good and the bad seed. Both suggest the complexity of life and the inevitability of evil as well as good in the world and in the church. Both call for a certain tolerance now in the conviction that in the end there will be a judgment and a separating of the two.

The first two parables obviously form a pair. They both affirm the extraordinary nature of the gift offered us in Jesus and point to the kind of response that those who recognize it are called to make. The kingdom is like a treasure hidden in a field or like a pearl of great value; whoever discovers it should be willing in joy to give up everything in order to possess it.

Seeking and Finding

The two parables are extremely simple. No explanation is needed or given. The human experiences they evoke are easily understood. A person comes upon a particularly beautiful work of art or a rare book or a house with a breathtaking view. For those who have eyes for such things, a "find" like these can motivate them to any and every sacrifice in order to obtain it.

The kingdom as preached by Jesus is God himself turned to

149

us in love and forgiveness. To discover God is to discover meaning and purpose; it is to be filled with a sense of peace and of joy. Sometimes we go out actively searching for such values; sometimes they encounter us by surprise on our journey. In either case our response should be the same.

Those who recognize the presence and the value of the kingdom are willing to make sacrifices for it. They are willing to give time to it and above all to abandon everything in their life that would undermine or contradict it.

Discerning Good from Evil

The wonderful story in today's first reading suggests the kind of qualities that are needed if we are to recognize and respond to the gift of the kingdom. The young Solomon has just succeeded to the throne of Israel after his father David. He realizes his youth and inexperience and when in a dream God asks him what he wants he answers: an attentive or listening heart and an ability to discern between good and evil.

Solomon seeks wisdom, a wisdom to understand people and situations and a judgment to know how to respond to them. He asks for the heart and mind of a true and just leader. God marvels at the maturity of his request and promises him a wise and discerning mind. The word in Hebrew here is really heart. For the Bible wisdom involves an intellectual dimension but even more a moral and intuitive one, a sensitive and feeling heart.

If we are to recognize and cooperate with God's presence in our life and in our world we too will need an attentive heart and a discerning mind. Wisdom both human and religious is essential if we are to respond to the coming of God's reign among us.

Conformed to Christ

In today's second reading Paul suggests one way that we might think about what such a response entails. Called by God to become sisters and brothers of Christ, we are to be conformed to or like him in all that we do. This has been God's plan for us from before the beginning of time.

Paul affirms that everything works together for good for those who love God. The most important thing for Paul as for Jesus is that we recognize the presence of God in our life and that we respond to God's call with generosity and courage. If we do so, then no matter what happens to us, no matter what we might have to suffer, no matter how restricted our scope for doing good might be, we can be confident that our life will be meaningful and that it will contribute to the coming of God's kingdom.

As always, Paul's message is one of hope and trust. God has called us in Christ and he will be faithful to that call. Having justified us he will bring us to fulfillment in eternal glory. Being even now in Christ we know that we are destined to share his heavenly life. To be sisters and brothers of Jesus is not for a moment or for a day but for all eternity.

Compassionate Love

18TH SUNDAY IN ORDINARY TIME
Readings: Is 55:1-3, Rom 8:35, 37-39, Mt 14:13-21

Today's gospel contains the well-known story of the multiplication of the loaves and fish. Striking is the implied contrast evoked by the reference to the death of John the Baptist. While the banquet at which Herod presided was marked by lust, jealousy and violence, the meal to which Jesus invites the crowd and us celebrates and expresses compassionate love.

On seeing the crowd gathered on the shore of the lake Jesus has compassion on them. He is touched in particular by the many sick people who have been brought to him and he heals them. The same compassion later leads him to instruct the disciples to feed the throng. What is happening here is much more than a temporary alleviation of hunger. It is a tangible manifestation of God's continuing love and compassion for human beings.

The reference to the deserted place evokes the story of the people of Israel in the wilderness when God nourished them with the gift of manna. The description of Jesus blessing, breaking and distributing the bread looks forward to the last supper and to the eucharist. All these different events reveal the compassionate love of God, a love that is now focused for us in Jesus.

Listen and Live

It is the same compassion that is evoked and celebrated in today's first reading. In a prophetic oracle the Lord invites those who hunger and thirst to come to him and to eat and drink. He chides those who waste their money on unimportant things and promises to give their fill to those who are poor.

Surprising in the passage is the emphasis on listening. "Incline your ear," the Lord says, "listen so that you may live." If the initial reference is to real food and real drink, they are to be understood also as sacraments or signs of a deeper and more fundamental kind of food. What ultimately we hunger and thirst for and what finally God is offering us is himself.

The text speaks of "an everlasting covenant" and refers to God's steadfast love for David. The God of the Bible is a God of liberation and of salvation, a God who hears and responds to the cry of the poor. In all of this he has shown himself, in the words of today's psalm, as kind and full of compassion, as close to all who call on him from their hearts.

The Love of Christ

Paul experienced the compassion and the love of God in his own conversion. Reconciliation, healing, justification came to him not because of any merit on his part but entirely as a result of God's graciousness. In today's reading from Romans Paul proclaims his great confidence and trust in the love of God and of Christ of which he knows himself to be the recipient.

Preaching the gospel was not always easy for Paul. It brought persecution and hardship, imprisonment and the jealousy of other preachers. Nothing, however, was able to sway him from his course. He remains convinced that nothing will ever separate him from the love of Christ. Here is the source of that strength and courage which allow him to triumph over all adversity.

To believe in God and in God's love revealed to us through Christ is to have all one needs to become a truly free person. In the light of such faith nothing else has ultimate significance. Nothing can deny, destroy or in any way undermine the compassionate love of God poured into our hearts through the gift of Christ's Spirit.

A Compassionate People

Made in God's image and likeness we are called to be like God, to reflect in our own lives the compassion and love that define his being. As followers of Jesus we are invited to imitate his example and to live according to his Spirit.

Jesus had compassion on people in need and especially on the sick. Although we do not have miraculous power we can reach out to those who suffer. Over the centuries medicine has tried to understand and counteract the many diseases and disasters that threaten our bodily existence. In spite of scientific and technological progress, the sick still need compassion and love. They need people who can empathize with them and reach out to them in their isolation and pain.

The feeding of the five thousand evokes the eucharist and the desire of Jesus to feed us with the bread of life. If the eucharistic bread stills spiritual hunger, it is not meant to distract us from but rather to alert us to the physical hunger that so many suffer. In having compassion on those who were hungry, Jesus invites and challenges us to do the same.

It Is I

19TH SUNDAY IN ORDINARY TIME
Readings: 1 Kgs 19:9a, 11-13a, Rom 9:1-5, Mt 14:22-33

Matthew's account of the coming of Jesus across the water to the disciples in their storm-tossed boat emphasizes what the incident reveals about the mysterious depths of Jesus' person. He tells the story in the form of a theophany, a manifestation of the presence in Jesus of God's merciful and saving power.

Mark's account of the same event ends with the disciples in a state of astonished confusion. They do not understand, he tells us, for their hearts are hardened. Matthew's version is a great deal more positive. The power that Jesus exercises over wind and wave convinces the disciples that he is indeed the Son of God. And so they fall down before him in adoration.

Echoing in his own way Mark's more ambivalent portrayal of the disciples, Matthew includes a brief episode that focuses on Peter. It reveals in him and by extension in the disciples as a whole a paradoxical presence of both belief and unbelief. In a manner typical of him, Peter brashly calls on Jesus to invite him to walk toward him across the water. Almost as soon as he leaves the safety of the boat Peter becomes frightened and begins to sink. Jesus rebukes him as a person of "little faith."

A Sound of Silence

The idea of a theophany or manifestation of God is central to biblical religion. God is not simply the distant and hidden creator of the world but someone who is close to and involved in it. He cares about all of creation and takes an active and saving interest in human history.

The manifestation of God to Moses in the burning bush began the story of the exodus and of the sealing of the covenant at

Sinai. Today's first reading evokes those earlier events even as it points to the presence of God in a still more mysterious way. Rejected by Israel's rulers, Elijah has withdrawn into the desert to the mountain of God. There he awaits God's revelation.

Thunder and lightning, earthquake and fire were the natural forces that people at the time most spontaneously associated with God. On this occasion, however, it is not in them that the prophet discerns God's presence but in a sound of utter silence. The phrase has become a favored one with mystics of all ages. When the noise of human language and of nature subsides, God's word begins to sound in the silence of our hearts.

For the Sake of My People

If today's gospel reveals a conflict in Peter between faith and doubt, the second reading exemplifies the kind of conflict that real faith sometimes brings in its wake. The text begins a long section of three chapters in the letter to the Romans in which Paul reflects on the vocation and identity of Israel.

The first Christians, like Paul, were all Jews. They recognized in Jesus the Christ of Israel, the fulfillment of their hopes and longings. As the years passed and many of their co-religionists did not accept the new faith, they asked themselves why. No one struggled with this question more personally or more intensely than Paul. He speaks of the "great sorrow and unceasing anguish" that the issue calls forth in his heart.

Paul begins by recalling the prerogatives that belong to the Jews as God's chosen people, as those to whom God gave the law and revealed his glory, as those with whom he sealed a covenant and entrusted the promises. None of this can be taken from them.

The Experience of God

For many people in our largely secular world, the loving presence and even the very existence of God are far from self-evident. Surrounded by the products of our own hands and acutely aware of responsibility for ourselves and others, we easily become insensitive to our radical dependence on God.

Karl Rahner, a Jesuit theologian and spiritual writer, published fifty years ago a small volume of prayers entitled *Encounters with Silence*. The prayers are as fresh today and as hauntingly contemporary as when he wrote them. They reflect a modern and yet very traditional sense of the healing, life-giving nearness of God as well as of the inevitable darkness and mystery in which that nearness is shrouded.

God is as near to us as we are to ourselves. We need to be silent and to listen to the mystery that wells up within us and that in those events and experiences that challenge and touch us breaks through the surface of our everyday life. It is revealed in our creativity and our longing, in our sense of limits and of moral responsibility. God is the ultimate ground and silent partner of all our efforts to become truly loving persons.

Jews and Gentiles

20TH SUNDAY IN ORDINARY TIME
**Readings: Is 56:1, 6-7, Rom 11:13-15, 29-32,
Mt 15:21-28**

The identities and destinies of Judaism and Christianity are inseparable. Jesus himself was a first century Palestinian Jew whose religious and human sensitivities and language were steeped in the history and traditions of his people. As today's gospel reminds us, his mission and ministry were restricted to "the lost sheep of the house of Israel." He never presented himself as the founder of a new religion but rather as someone announcing to his fellow Jews that the God of their history, the God of creation and of exodus, was active in him, offering salvation and calling them to conversion and newness of life.

After the resurrection the initial preaching of the gospel was directed to Jews. It was only gradually and in the face of the partial failure of the Jewish mission that the apostles turned to the Gentiles. Before long Paul and others were arguing that such people in becoming Christians did not need to embrace the Jewish law. Salvation, they said, was not through the works of the law but through faith in Jesus Christ. It was this conviction that gradually over several decades led to the predominantly Gentile Christianity that we now take for granted.

A Canaanite Woman

If Jesus' public life was largely confined to the world of Palestinian Judaism, the gospels do contain a few references to encounters of various kinds with Gentiles. Today's text recounts one of the best known and touching of such incidents.

Tyre and Sidon, situated on the Mediterranean coast, were places with a predominantly Gentile population. A Canaanite woman, someone issued from the old pagan stock that predated the arrival of the Israelites in the area, approaches Jesus and begs him to cure her daughter. The disciples rebuke her but she persists. When Jesus quotes a proverb about not throwing the food of children to dogs, she accepts the rather insulting identification of pagans with dogs but says that even they are allowed to eat the crumbs that fall from the master's table.

Jesus' rather lavish praise for the faith of the woman made it easier for the apostles and others to respond positively when Gentiles began to welcome their message. The incident seemed to warrant a spreading of the gospel beyond the confines of Judaism.

A House of Prayer for All Peoples

Central to Israel's experience from an early date was a sense of being called by God to become in a special way his people. The covenant emphasized the exclusive commitment that Israel was to make in return. In the name of that commitment various prophets at different times in biblical history insisted on the separation that ought to exist between Jews and others. It was thought in certain circumstances to be the only way in which they could maintain the purity of their religious lives.

Today's first reading, taken from the latter part of the book of Isaiah, strikes a different note. It hints at some kind of universalism. The emphasis is not on missionary outreach but rather on the welcome that God extends to foreigners who live in the midst of the Jewish people and who take part in their religious traditions and practices. Their prayers and sacrifices are acceptable. In the day of the Lord, Jew and Gentile will worship side by side. Then all will know that the temple is meant to be "a house of prayer for all peoples."

Merciful to All

The person more than any other who contributed to the opening of Christianity to the Gentiles was the apostle Paul. As an educated and committed Jew he subsequently agonized over the fact that while some Jews accepted Jesus as the messiah, many others did not. In the very letter in which he develops at some length his understanding of justification by faith in Christ, he also dedicates three chapters to the question of the Jews and of their continuing relationship with God. It is from the third of these chapters that today's second reading is drawn.

What Paul finally comes up against is the mystery of God's ways with us. No one can justify himself or herself. We all depend on God's grace and mercy. Had all the Jews accepted the gospel, the end times might have come. Because they did not, a new phase in history began creating for Gentiles an opportunity to respond to the gospel. Paul cannot believe that God has withdrawn his gifts from Israel. In fact he hopes that in the end all Jews will come to recognize Jesus for who he is. For now Gentile Christians should cherish their own Jewish roots and have respect for the continuing place of Israel in God's plan of salvation.

Who Am I?

21ST SUNDAY IN ORDINARY TIME
Readings: Is 22:15, 19-23, Rom 11:33-36, Mt 16:13-20

The well-known incident that constitutes today's gospel is dramatically told. Having come into the district of Caesarea Philippi, a region associated in Israel's past with divine revelation, Jesus confronts the disciples with the question of his identity. They have heard him preach, seen his miracles, shared his way of life. Given all that, who do they think he is?

Jesus begins indirectly by asking what others are saying about him. Clearly he has raised expectations and provoked discussion. Recognizing something extraordinary in him, people are beginning to wonder whether he is one or other of the great prophetic figures of Israel come back to life. Such views are anything but negative, and yet they fall short of the mark.

And so Jesus asks: Who do you say that I am? It is a question that has haunted believers and unbelievers ever since. That Jesus was a remarkable person, a person of faith and courage, of integrity and sensitivity, that he reached out in a compassionate and fearless way to those on the margins of society, is clear. But what was and is his ultimate identity?

The Son of the Living God

Here, as so often in the gospels, it is Simon Peter who speaks on behalf of the others. He affirms that Jesus is the messiah, the anointed one of Israel. The Greek word for this is "Christos" or Christ. Although there were different views among Jews at the time about the messiah, all saw him as coming from God and as bringing into the world definitive salvation.

With time, the disciples will gradually learn what is distinctive about Jesus' messiahship. He comes not to rule but to serve.

His way includes rejection and suffering and death. The meaning of the messianic title is modified here by the phrase that accompanies it. Jesus is "the Son of the living God."

Over the centuries Peter's profession of faith became a focus of Christian reflection and prayer and eventually yielded up, in conjunction with the rest of the New Testament, the classical formulations of Christian faith in the unique presence of God in Jesus. He is Son of God in a way in which no one else has been or ever will be.

Revealed by God

Alone among the evangelists, Matthew includes in his account of Caesarea Philippi the response of Jesus to Peter. In declaring Peter blessed, he accepts the truth of his profession. He insists, however, that it was not due to Peter's own intelligence or insight or moral goodness. It came as a revelation from God and as such it was meant not just for Peter but for the church that would be rooted in his faith and testimony.

Jesus' answer to Peter contains a remarkable promise. The gates of Hades, that is, the power of death and of the underworld, will never overwhelm the community of Jesus' disciples. At the end of Matthew's gospel Jesus assures the disciples that he will be with them until the end of time.

Peter himself is given a special role in the community, a role analogous to that of Eliakim in today's first reading. There Isaiah announces that the steward will be entrusted with the keys over the royal household. Peter is promised the keys of the kingdom of heaven. Implied in this is a responsibility of religious leadership that throughout history has been exercised in the church by bishops and in a special way by the pope.

How Inscrutable His Ways

Today's second reading is a hymn to the creator God and to his saving yet hidden ways with us. In its original context in Romans it refers specifically to the relationship between Israel and the world of the Gentiles and to the ways in which God uses both for the salvation of all. If this is the immediate reference, the message of the hymn has a universal import.

God is the beginning and end of our lives and of all that exists. Everything comes from and is sustained by God and has him as its ultimate goal. To believe in God is to believe in the dignity and value of creation and in the meaningfulness of our lives and of human history. In spite of sin and suffering God's plan for us and for creation is gradually being fulfilled.

The coming of Jesus helps us to understand and to relate creatively to God's plan of salvation. Although his ways remain inscrutable, we are given some sense of them in the destiny of Jesus. He calls us to love and fidelity. When God's ways entail the cross and suffering, we are to embrace even these, for in them God's wisdom continues to unfold. To him be glory forever.

A Living Sacrifice

22ND SUNDAY IN ORDINARY TIME
Readings: Jer 20:7-9, Rom 12:1-2, Mt 16:21-27

Today's brief second reading uses a traditional image to evoke and give expression to what is in fact the deepest dimension of the Christian life. Paul encourages us to offer our bodies, our selves, to God as a living sacrifice. This, he says, is the kind of worship that God asks of us, the worship that corresponds to our nature as spiritual beings made in God's image and likeness.

The sacrifice of animals and of the fruits of the earth was widely practiced in antiquity and was a central element in the liturgy of the great temple in Jerusalem. Evoking that background, Paul affirms that what God wants from us finally is not things but ourselves. We have come from God; we belong to God; ultimately we and all of creation will return to him.

We are to give ourselves to God not only by worshiping him in prayer but also by the way we live, by our efforts to do what is right and just and good. If we are to live in such a way, Paul says, we cannot simply be carried along by the concerns and values of contemporary culture. We need to discern God's will for us, and, in order to do that, our minds need to be renewed.

Human or Divine Thoughts

Today's gospel underlines how difficult it can be for us to undergo the kind of renewal that Paul believes is so necessary. For the first time Jesus begins to talk to the disciples about his coming rejection and death. Peter's reaction is swift and negative. As much as it reveals a certain generosity of spirit on his part, it provokes from Jesus a stern rebuke.

The rock upon which Jesus has said that he will build his church has become a stumbling block. Peter's reaction is one-sidedly human. He is not yet open in any adequate manner to the mysterious and paradoxical ways of God. In his revulsion at the thought of Jesus' failure, Peter is doing the work of Satan, the tempter, the adversary of God and of God's saving activity.

Universalizing the lesson of his own life, Jesus announces that the paradox of the cross must be the way of all his disciples. There is in all of us an element of self-destructiveness that sets us at odds with God. Authentic human life always entails a conversion, a letting go of a certain kind of egoism and an opening of the self to the will and to the gift of God.

A Fire in My Bones

Today's first reading exemplifies in a dramatic fashion the struggles that religiously sensitive persons can undergo in trying to respond to God's will. As special as Jeremiah's vocation was, it throws light on the profoundly personal nature of the relationship with God to which we are all called.

In spite of hesitations Jeremiah had accepted the vocation of prophet. It soon brought him, however, rejection and scorn. His message was not what his contemporaries were looking for. They wanted encouragement and affirmation, not warning and condemnation. Their response was violence and anger.

As much as Jeremiah wanted and even attempted to remain silent, he was unable. God's word within him was like a burning fire. He tried to deny it, repress it, hold it in, but he could not. His experience has been echoed repeatedly in the lives of saints and others who have been led in the face of enormous difficulties to commit themselves to some ideal or some group of people. When such commitment is for the good we can be sure that it is rooted in the presence of God's Spirit.

Pleasing to God

All three of today's readings suggest the energy and vitality, the struggle and effort involved in trying to live one's life in the presence of the living God. Our God is not distant but near. He is not a blind force but a personal reality, a true Thou, who calls us into relationship with him.

In baptism we are all graced with the gift of God's Spirit and are invited to embrace a vocation involving a personal relationship with God. This relationship is be worked out in the midst of the concrete things and concerns that constitute our everyday life. Everything we do brings us closer to God or drives us further away from him.

In the eucharist we praise and worship God and seek his blessing. We open ourselves to the gift of Jesus and enter into his act of self-giving love. In all of this we bring the hope and despair, the joy and sorrow, the success and failure, that constitute our life. With them we bring ourselves so that our lives may be ever more truly a living sacrifice pleasing to God.

Love and Reconciliation

23RD SUNDAY IN ORDINARY TIME
Readings: Ezek 33:7-9, Rom 13:8-10, Mt 18:15-20

Today's gospel deals with what must have been a delicate and difficult situation within the small communities of early Christianity. People knew one another and were deeply affected, positively and negatively, by the way that individual believers acted. Jesus speaks of the case where one of the disciples has sinned in some obvious fashion and in doing so has threatened the life of the community. His first concern is that every effort should be made to win back the sinner, to reach out to him or her a hand of reconciliation. If the person refuses to respond, then other steps are to be taken until finally, if necessary, the guilty party is to be cut off from the community.

The language in Matthew's account of the incident has a somewhat juridical or legal ring to it. Specific rules are established for handling conflict and division. What ultimately is at stake, however, is a deeply religious reality. The community exercises judgment in the name of God and therefore in doing so its members must turn to him in prayer. If they do, they can be sure that God will hear them and support them in their efforts to renew and heal community life.

I Am Among You

The passage concludes with a remarkable promise. Jesus says that where two or three are gathered in his name he will be there among them. The immediate context is obviously that of the judgment to be made about how to handle a recalcitrant sinner, but the implications of the saying are much broader. Christian life is life in Christ. Through faith and baptism and through the gift of the Spirit, we all share in the life of Jesus. When we pray together and when we talk together in his name about issues that affect him and our relationship to him, we are not alone. If we open ourselves to his inspiration, there is every reason to hope that our decisions will reflect his will.

Today's first reading has obvious parallels with the gospel. It speaks of Ezekiel as a watchman or sentinel whose task it is to warn those who have gone astray. If he fails to do so, then, when God's punishment comes upon them, he will have to share in it. The message for us, once again, is that we are all responsible for one another. We cannot turn away in indifference from what we recognize as sinful and destructive behavior in others.

Love One Another

In today's second reading Paul argues that love of neighbor represents the fulfillment of the Mosaic law. The ten commandments as they apply to our relationship to others forbid a series of fundamental human wrongs. Love, Paul says, does no wrong to others and by that very fact guarantees the fulfillment of what the law asks of us in our relationships with one another.

Love, of course, does much more than avoid evil. It is a positive impulse that seeks what is good. When we really love others, we want to be good to them, help them in any way we can, give things to them. In the case of Jesus love impelled him to lay down his life for our salvation.

Most of us learn to love in our families and in our relations with friends. What Jesus asks of us is to reach out beyond our immediate circles and bring an attitude of love to all those with whom we come in contact. Obviously we cannot have the same intensity of feeling and concern for everyone, but we can learn gradually to avoid what harms them and to do what helps them.

A Christian Community

There is a widespread sense that the Christian person is the loving person, the kind and good and gentle person, the one who in real self-forgetfulness reaches out to and helps those in need. As often as this ideal in our society is watered down and robbed of its religious roots, this perception remains a striking witness to much of what in fact the gospel teaches.

A full Christian life, however, involves other things as well, beginning with faith in God turned to us in Jesus Christ and active among us in the power of the Spirit. Such faith draws us into the community of the church and propels us to praise and worship God and to share actively in the eucharist. Such faith also demands a way of life modeled on the example of Jesus.

If love of neighbor is the fulfillment of the law, then love should be the distinguishing characteristic of every Christian community, whether it be family, school, parish or diocese. We are not to harm others but to do them good. When we ourselves fail we can only hope that someone will reach out to us and draw us back into the communities to which we belong.

Mercy and Forgiveness

24TH SUNDAY IN ORDINARY TIME
Readings: Sir 27:30–28:7, Rom 14:7-9, Mt 18:21-35

True forgiveness is rarely easy. Recent history reveals once again how difficult it is across racial, national and cultural boundaries. It can be every bit as challenging in regard to friends or family members. We tend to harbor hurts and slights and to react to the least disregard or wrong.

Peter probably thought he was being generous in asking whether he should be ready to forgive seven times. Jesus disagreed. Whether the word he used in answer should be translated seventy-seven times or seventy times seven, his view is clear. Forgiveness is to be without limits. The parable that he tells suggests why.

The contrast between the amount of money owed to the king and to his slave or servant is deliberately exaggerated. There is no possible way that the latter could ever pay back the enormous debt he owes his master. What his fellow slave owes him, on the other hand, is relatively little. The contrast underlines both the callousness of the first slave and his blindness to the extraordinary mercy he has received.

So God Will Do to Us

When the king learns what his servant has done, he is justly outraged and casts him into prison. A man as small-minded and petty as this servant deserves no mercy. He will be treated as he treated his fellow slave. And so, Jesus adds, will God treat us if we do not forgive others from our heart.

The parable illustrates in dramatic form a principle enunciated in the sermon on the mount. There after teaching the disciples the Our Father, Jesus added: "If you forgive others their trespasses, your heavenly Father will also forgive you; but if you do not forgive others, neither will your Father forgive your trespasses." The parable reverses the order of what Jesus had earlier said and argues that because God has revealed himself in our regard as a God of mercy and forgiveness we ought to imitate him in our relations to one another.

A conviction about the relation between forgiving others and the hope of forgiveness from God is a part of the wisdom tradition of Israel. Today's first reading recognizes how natural to us anger and the desire for vengeance are, and yet it affirms that if we want God's forgiveness, we must forgive those who wrong us.

Mercy for One Like Yourself

True forgiveness, the kind that rises up from the depths of the heart, is not something that is always in our power. We know sometimes that we should forgive and at some level really want to but are unable. This happens particularly with those who are near to us, a parent or child, a divorced spouse or former friend. The hurt that has been done remains so deep that, until it is to some degree healed, forgiveness is all but impossible.

Jesus is not denying the complexity of our emotions or the process that we might have to go through before being able to forgive. He is saying that we must not act on our anger and by so doing continue the circle of violence or hurt that has begun.

Sirach speaks of having mercy on someone like oneself. We all share a common humanity. Forgiveness becomes easier as we begin to understand those who hurt us, understand what has made them the way that they are. This does not mean accepting evil and pain but it does mean achieving the kind of insight that eventually will make mercy and forgiveness possible.

To Live to the Lord

In today's second reading Paul insists that as believers we are not simply to live for and by ourselves but rather in relationship to Jesus Christ. Life today for many involves loneliness and isolation. Having little sense of roots, our culture offers scant help to those struggling to establish or deepen a sense of identity. Christianity affirms the reality of our spiritual roots. It anchors our identity in that of Christ.

Jesus embodied mercy and forgiveness. He did not condone evil nor did he turn a blind eye to what was destructive in the way that people acted. He challenged it, and because he did he was eventually put to death. And yet he forgave. He forgave from the cross as he forgave so often during his life.

Mercy and forgiveness become easier as we become more identified with Christ. In him we realize the depths of the love and mercy shown us by God. As our hearts are transformed by the Spirit of Jesus, we cannot help but become more like him. True mercy and forgiveness are not the result of a day or a year but of a lifetime of human experience and of growth in Christ.

Extravagant Generosity

25TH SUNDAY IN ORDINARY TIME
Readings: Is 55:6-9, Phil 1:20c-24, 27, Mt 20:1-16

The insight into God's relationship to us offered by the parable in today's gospel is surprising and encouraging and to some degree a little disturbing. God's generosity and mercy know no bounds. Their manifestation, however, is not always understood. In many ways the parable of "the good employer" evokes thoughts and feelings analogous to those we experience on hearing the parable of the prodigal son.

The story Jesus tells is meant to throw light on the kingdom of God or of heaven. It suggests the way that God is present in Jesus and what it is that he is doing through him. The landowner or householder hires day laborers to work in his vineyard and agrees with them on a reasonable salary. He is a just man and at the end of the day he pays what he has promised. What is surprising is not his justice but his mercy.

As in the case of the prodigal's elder brother, we cannot help but sympathize with the workers who have sweated all day in the blazing sun and yet who receive the same wage as those who labored but a single hour. From our point of view, they have every right to grumble. And yet they are reprimanded.

Abounding in Love

It is more than likely that Jesus told this parable in order to defend himself and his activity. The religious leaders of the day attacked him for eating with tax collectors and sinners, for bringing himself into contact with people who from a strict religious point of view were outcasts and untouchables. Jesus' answer to his critics is that he is doing God's work.

Today's first reading offers a striking parallel to the gospel.

The passage is from the last chapter of the so-called book of consolation in the second part of Isaiah. The prophet invites people to seek God, to turn to him. No matter who they are or what they have done, if they allow themselves to be converted, God will embrace them with mercy and pardon.

The text contains an oracle announcing that God is radically different from us. As the heavens transcend the earth, it says, so God's thoughts and ways go beyond anything we can imagine. What is affirmed here is more than God's incomprehensibility. Isaiah is proclaiming the depths of the riches of divine mercy and love. Jesus' parable suggests that the same mercy has become active in a new and surprising way in his life and preaching.

Worthy of the Gospel

If the emphasis in today's parable, as in so much of the teaching of Jesus, is on the mercy of God, that mercy brings with it its own demands. Those who worked the full day are chided for failing to appreciate the employer's generosity. We have to learn to think not of ourselves but of God's mercy and rejoice in what it accomplishes among people everywhere.

In today's second reading Paul encourages the Christians at Philippi to strive to live a life worthy of the gospel of Christ. Paul knows that he and they have been the recipients of God's merciful grace but he also knows that God's gift is meant to bear fruit. Those who accept Jesus' message of the kingdom are to become his disciples and imitate his way of life.

Paul is writing in the midst of persecution and suffering. In spite of everything, he is convinced that Christ is with him and that his presence will be visible in all that he does in Christ's name. For Paul, to live is Christ, while to die is simply to be with Christ in a new and more intense way.

God Is Near

In their different ways, all of today's readings affirm the presence of God in the midst of our lives. Rooted in a love and mercy that go beyond anything we can imagine, God's presence is surprising and sometimes disturbing in the way that it bursts ordinary expectations and opens new possibilities and vistas. The biblical God, the God proclaimed and revealed in the life and destiny of Jesus, is not distant but near. He is with us in our individual and collective histories, offering us his love and forgiveness and calling us to new forms of generosity.

The parable of the laborers in the vineyard or of the generous and merciful employer invites us to recognize God's mercy and to rejoice in and accept it into our own lives. At the same time it challenges us to be sensitive to and respectful of what God in his compassion is doing in the lives of others. If extravagant generosity is the key to the identity of the God who is revealed in Jesus, then generosity of spirit should be a mark of everyone who strives to lead a life worthy of his gospel.

The Mind of Christ

26TH SUNDAY IN ORDINARY TIME
Readings: Ezek 18:25-28, Phil 2:1-11, Mt 21:28-32

In today's second reading, Paul appeals to believers at Philippi and through them to Christians everywhere to develop a community life worthy of the gospel of Christ. We are not to live our faith as isolated individuals, he reminds us, but as members of Christ's body. Our coming together, therefore, should be marked not by ambition or self-seeking, but by a genuine desire for mutual understanding and service. A community built on love demands as a condition of its possibility humility and a certain self-forgetfulness.

One way of formulating what is required is to say that we must have the mind, the attitude, the ways of thinking and feeling, that were in Christ. To spell out what this means, Paul quotes what may well have been an already existing hymn. It tells the story of Jesus in broad but powerful strokes. His whole life, from his mysterious birth to his scandalous and brutal death on the cross, was marked by humility and self-emptying. Although in the form of God, he entered into the depths of human existence and embraced it in all its brokenness and confusion, including the impenetrable darkness of death.

God Exalted Him

In spite of the emphasis on self-emptying, the hymn ends on a triumphant note. Because Jesus fulfilled his human destiny in total obedience to God's will, his death became a threshold to glory. Raising him to the fullness of life, God gave him a share in the divine name so that now every knee is to bend before him and every tongue confess that he is Lord.

To have the mind of Christ is, on one level, to imitate him.

Discipleship implies following Jesus, seeking in his way of living and acting a pattern for one's own life. The phrase "in Christ," however, suggests something more. Through faith and baptism, we share in Christ's life; he lives in us and we in him. To have the mind of Christ, in this sense, is to allow oneself to be molded by Christ's Spirit from within.

In the eucharist Jesus is present precisely in his act of self-giving love. In celebrating and sharing in it we are invited and enabled in an ever deepening fashion to put on his mind, to become like him. As we reflect on his example, we are inspired by his Spirit to put it into practice.

Saying and Doing

Today's gospel shows Jesus in a situation of conflict with the religious leaders of his time. In the face of their challenge to his authority, he manifests the tenuousness of their own position. He puts a question to them in the form of a parable. Who are truly good, those who say that they intend to do good but do not or those who say they will not but in fact do?

The application that Jesus makes of the parable is specific and paradoxical. The chief priests and elders belong to the first group while the second group includes tax collectors and prostitutes. Jesus is not claiming that people are good or bad simply because of their background or profession. He is pointing rather to the surprising ways in which people often act.

Jesus bases his judgment on his contemporaries on the actual way in which they responded to John the Baptist's preaching. By implication he is also referring to their reaction to him. Before God, status and reputation count for nothing. The quality of one's life determines one's relation to the kingdom.

Repent and Live

Today's brief first reading is from a chapter in Ezekiel dealing with the issue of personal responsibility. The prophet rejects the proverb: "The parents have eaten sour grapes and the children's teeth are set on edge." Children are not to be punished for the sins of their parents or vice versa. Before God everyone is responsible for his or her own actions.

The passage focuses in particular on the phenomenon of good people who turn bad and of sinners who undergo a conversion. In both cases, the last situation of the person will be the basis for judgment. The whole chapter culminates in a pressing invitation to conversion. "Turn and live."

As strong and condemnatory as Jesus' language to the chief priests and elders is, it too includes a call to conversion. If up to this point they have not responded to God's call, there is still time to do so. Conversion, moreover, is never complete. Paul in the second reading is writing to people who are already Christians. In urging them to put on the mind of Christ, he is asking them to continue a process which they have already begun.

God's Vineyard

27TH SUNDAY IN ORDINARY TIME
Readings: Is 5:1-7, Phil 4:6-9, Mt 21:33-43

The imagery of the vineyard and grapes and more generally of the fruits of the earth recurs regularly throughout the Bible. Both the first and the third readings today compare God's people to a vineyard. In the gospel Jesus directs a rather pointed parable at the religious leaders of his time, accusing them of failure in their responsibilities in regard to God's vineyard.

Unlike most of the parables of Jesus, this one invites, at least to some degree, an allegorical interpretation. The slaves whom the landowner sends at harvest time to collect his share of the produce and who are maltreated and put to death make one think of the prophets. The son, on the other hand, who is cast out of the vineyard and then killed clearly refers to Jesus and to the death he suffered outside of the walls of Jerusalem.

When chided by Jesus, even the chief priests and the elders have to admit that the actions of the tenants are unacceptable. In condemning them, however, they unwittingly condemn themselves. The kingdom, Jesus says, and their responsibilities in regard to it, will be taken from them and given to others who will produce fruit worthy of God's gift.

A Song of Love

In the first reading Isaiah begins what in fact is a parable by calling it a love song. He speaks of his beloved who lavished enormous care and attention on his vineyard. He did everything possible to make it fertile and safe and planted in it only the very best vines. Imagine his disappointment when it produced not good but wild grapes, rotten grapes, grapes sour to the taste.

Embittered by his experience, he decides to abandon the

vineyard, to let weeds and wild animals overrun and destroy it. God's reaction to our failure to bear good fruit in our lives, Isaiah says, is similar. The vineyard is God's people and what God wants from them is justice and goodness but what he finds is violence and bloodshed and the anguished cry of the oppressed.

There is a sense in which all of creation is a love song. God called us and all that is into existence in an act of utter self-giving love. He wants us to bear fruit, to become decent and loving people and to create the kind of world in which justice will flourish and peace will be enjoyed by all. How far this is from the world as it actually exists is only too obvious.

The God of Peace

In his letter to the Philippians, Paul has spoken of his own imprisonment and suffering on behalf of the gospel as well as of certain embittered and embittering conflicts dividing the community. As he nears the end of the letter he begs his readers not to allow such things or their own personal concerns to rob them of their joy and peace. No matter what their situation or their failings, if they can but turn in prayer to God they will experience again that peace of God that goes beyond all understanding, that peace that has become theirs through Jesus Christ.

As important, however, as prayer is, Paul goes on to insist, it must be accompanied by a sincere effort to live a life of discipleship. Using the language of the philosophy of his day, Paul encourages his readers to opt for what is true and honorable, pure and just. Over and above all these things, they are to put into practice everything that they have learned from his teaching and example.

To Bear Fruit

All three readings are one in their challenge and encouragement to us to lead a life worthy of the gospel. God's love story with humanity, like every love story, demands reciprocity and mutuality. Love presupposes freedom and involves commitment. In creating us in his own image and likeness, God has made us free, has given us a capacity to choose what is good, an ability to love not only created reality but God himself.

The last few verses of the second reading sum up the kind of fruit that God wants us to bear in our lives. It flows in large degree from who we are as human beings, from our social nature, from our responsibility for ourselves, our families, our cities and nations. To be alive at all is to be called to make a difference in the world, to contribute something to its betterment, to be honest and just, considerate and caring.

As people who have accepted in faith the gospel of Christ, we are called to keep alive its memory, to celebrate its reality, and to bear witness in our lives to its saving power. It is through prayer and the eucharist and through committed service to those in need that we bring forth the fruits of the kingdom.

The Lord's Table

28TH SUNDAY IN ORDINARY TIME
Readings: Is 25:6-10a, Phil 4:10-14, 19-20, Mt 22:1-14

In the parable in today's gospel Jesus once again compares the kingdom of God or of heaven to a festive meal, this time to a lavish banquet put on by a king to celebrate the wedding of his son. The image has very ancient biblical roots. In today's first reading Isaiah appeals to it in evoking the human and cosmic fulfillment that are to mark the end of time.

Mount Zion, Jerusalem, says the prophet, will be the scene of the triumph of all those from every nation who have sought God and trusted in him. He will prepare for them a rich banquet and take away once and for all the shroud of pain and sorrow that for so long has covered them. He will wipe away every tear from their faces and rob even death of its power.

To sit at the table of the Lord involves much more than having one's physical needs met. It means entering into communion with God, sharing in some way in God's life. The use of the banquet image to suggest what heaven or eternal life is all about underlines how in our return to God our desires and longings will be stilled and all our capacities will be brought to fulfillment.

Table Fellowship

If the kingdom of which Jesus spoke will reach its final state in eternal life, it is already present and active here and now. In all that Jesus said and did he proclaimed its presence and invited people to become a part of it. One of the more striking ways he did this was by sharing meals with them.

We are told on more than one occasion that Jesus ate with publicans and sinners and that his doing so provoked strong negative reactions from some of the religious leaders of the time.

They understood that Jesus' sitting down at table with such people was a parable in action proclaiming that God's kingdom was meant for them as well as for others.

Today's parable points to the meaning of such meals when it says that the king, having learned that those who were first invited refused to come, sent his servants out to the highways and crossroads to call people of any and every background. God's invitation in the end is universal. All that is required is that one come to the banquet dressed in a fitting robe. The reference here is clearly to the kind of moral and religious life implied in any serious following of Jesus.

The Eucharistic Table

The image of the meal takes on new meaning in relationship to the eucharist. The last supper presupposes the various gospel stories and parables about eating and table fellowship and gives them a new and deeper meaning. In identifying the shared bread and wine with himself, Jesus makes explicit the depths of the communion with him to which his followers are called.

The specific words that are said reveal the ultimate meaning of Jesus' life as an act of self-giving love. This is my body given for you, my blood poured out for your salvation. The eucharist is a continuing invitation to us to share in Jesus' life and in doing so to enter into communion with God.

In the eucharist we remember the life of Jesus, the meals that he shared with others, the stories that he told of final fulfillment, the love that brought him to the cross. Even as we remember him, however, and rejoice in his presence, we cannot help but look forward to our own final destiny in God. The eucharistic table is a promise of the eternal banquet.

All Things in Christ

Today's second reading is taken from near the end of Paul's letter to the Philippians. He expresses his joy and gratitude for the financial help they have been able to send to him as he languishes in prison. Even as he thanks them, however, he is anxious to share with them something of his inner life. If at one level he is obviously in need, at a deeper level he is not.

In a wonderful phrase, Paul sums up much of his Christian experience by saying that whether he has much or little, whether he is hungry or well fed, is finally of little consequence. His life is so rooted in Christ that he can cope with any situation, deal with any need. As true as this is, however, he remains touched by the kindness that they have shown to him.

The reading ends with a prayer and a doxology. Paul assures the Philippians that their generosity will be met and surpassed by the generosity of God. What they and Paul have done has been done to the praise and glory of God. They can all look forward to a final fulfillment when together they will share that glory forever and ever.

No Other Lord

29TH SUNDAY IN ORDINARY TIME
Readings: Is 45:1, 4-6, 1 Thess 1:1-5b, Mt 22:15-21

In the time of Jesus, Israel or Palestine, as it was then known, was part of the Roman empire and as such was subject to foreign rule and taxation. Not surprisingly Jewish reactions to this varied. Self-interest led some to collaborate actively with the Romans while others accepted their rule only grudgingly. A minority chafed under the Roman presence and plotted revolt.

The longer Jesus' public life went on, the more it tended to provoke negative reaction on the part of some of the leaders of the people. He was perceived as a threat both to their own positions and to the good order of society. And so they began to plot how they might embarrass him and in doing so either undermine his popular support or bring him into conflict with the authorities.

The question put to Jesus about whether or not it is lawful to pay taxes to the emperor represents a rather obvious trap. The questioners assume that no matter what his answer he will alienate at least one part of the people and perhaps even provoke the Romans. The tax referred to is a poll tax imposed on every subject of the empire and which had to be paid with a Roman coin.

The Things That Are God's

Jesus understands the motivation behind the question and instead of giving it an exhaustive answer deflects and frustrates the questioners in their purpose. The most widely circulated Roman denarius at the time bore the image of the emperor Tiberius and the inscription "Tiberius Caesar, august son of the divine Augustus, high priest." Paying the tax, Jesus says, is simply giving back to Caesar what already belongs to him.

Jesus refuses to be drawn into the trap. He is not a revolu-

185

tionary calling for rebellion against the Romans nor is he a collaborator seeking their support. His answer transforms the question by reminding his listeners that the real issue is not Caesar but God. We are to give to God what belongs to God.

Over the centuries Jesus' response has sometimes been used to justify a purely private and personal understanding of religion unrelated to political and social life. Such was certainly not its original meaning. For Jesus, God is the creator, the Lord of history, the origin and goal of all that is. Everything and everyone belong to God. No power or institution can claim exemption from God's will and purpose for human life.

No God Besides Me

Today's first reading underlines the universality of God's reach and interest. The prophet writes in the time of the exile and promises the people that God will soon intervene on their behalf. Our passage announces that this intervention will come through the hands of a non-Jew, Cyrus, king of the Persians. Because of the role he is to play in God's plan, he is called God's anointed or "messiah."

Even though Cyrus does not know the God of Israel, he has been chosen to bring about the return of the exiles to their homeland. God's will is worked through the larger political upheavals of the time. God is the Lord not only of human hearts and of his particular people but of all peoples and all history.

A true commitment to God and to the things of God can bring one into conflict with political and other structures of the world. Jesus proclaimed God's kingdom and called us to serve it by working for justice and peace and by reaching out to those most in need. In situations of oppression and poverty, this can involve opposition to the powers that be.

In God and in Christ

Today's second reading contains the opening lines of the oldest book of the New Testament, the first letter of Paul to the Thessalonians. The language is formal and highly structured and yet filled with rich theological content. Paul and two of his missionary companions send greetings of grace and peace to those believers at Thessalonica who have been brought together into a community of faith rooted in God and in Jesus.

Paul begins by giving thanks to God for the gifts of grace and life that have been bestowed upon the Thessalonians. He sums up their life by evoking what will become the classic triad of Christian virtues: faith, love and hope. The presence of such virtues in them is a sure sign that the grace of Christ is operative among them. Then as now the divine nature of the gospel message becomes clear in the power of the Spirit that accompanies its preaching. The greatest miracle remains steadfast faith and life-transforming love.

The Two Great Commandments

30TH SUNDAY IN ORDINARY TIME
Readings: Ex 22:21-27, 1 Thess 1:5c-10, Mt 22:34-40

Today's gospel reveals what, in the eyes of Jesus, is at the heart of all true morality and authentic religion. A Pharisee asks him which of the many commandments is the greatest. The answer is by no means self-evident. Later rabbis counted up 613 distinct positive and negative precepts in the Mosaic law.

In responding, Jesus brings together two passages from the Torah, Deuteronomy 6:5 and Leviticus 19:18. For Jesus, as for the whole of the biblical tradition, what God asks of us has repercussions on our relationship both with him and with one another. What is new in Jesus' answer and unique to his perspective is the juxtaposing of the two loves and the rooting of all our responsibilities in them.

The first of the great commandments has to with the love of God. We are to love God not in some vague and indefinite way but with all our heart and soul and mind. We are to love him, in other words, with all our being and with all that is within us. We are to dedicate to God and to the doing of God's will our emotional energy, our vitality and consciousness, our capacity to think and to plan.

Loving God with All Our Being

For Jesus, God is the great reality of his life and of all life. As much as God is beyond and other than all that we can know or imagine, Jesus teaches that God is near and is concerned about us. He wants to establish with us the most intimate of relationships. He loves us and invites us to love him in return.

It is not easy even to understand what loving God might mean. We cannot see God nor does he enter into our lives in the obvious and tangible ways in which other people do. And yet he is there, a silent partner of all our experiences, moving and drawing us beyond ourselves to him. God is the beginning and the end, the ground and the goal of all that we are and do. In Jesus God has been revealed as infinite and compassionate love.

John's gospel emphasizes that if we are called to love God, it is only because God has first loved us. Love is a gift that comes from God. We experience it in the form of God's Spirit alive and active within us. To love God with all our being is to be holy as God wants us to be holy. It is the work of a lifetime.

Loving Others as Ourselves

Jesus underlines that the second commandment is like the first and is its necessary complement. For many today, it may also be the way that first opens to them the possibility of loving God. Love in all its different forms is something that ought to come naturally to us and yet often does not. Here, again, our ability to love is ordinarily a result of the fact that we ourselves have been loved, by parents and by others.

Today's first reading contains examples of how concrete the commandments of the law were and suggests what Jesus means in saying that they all depend finally on the double command of love. We are not to oppress or do harm to those who are the most vulnerable among us, to those who because of background or family status or poverty are forced to live on the margins of society.

Echoing Jesus, Paul on two occasions sums up all the commandments with the phrase: "Love your neighbor as yourself." Love, he goes on to explain, does no wrong to anyone. If the avoidance of things like violence, anger, manipulation, and bad-mouthing does not exhaust what positively is meant by love, it does represent its necessary presupposition.

To Serve the Living God

In today's second reading Paul reminds the Thessalonians of their initial experience on hearing his preaching of the gospel. Because of their pagan background, what it brought to them first of all was a new sense of God and of God's relation to humanity. In Jesus, God was revealed as a living God, a God of life and of salvation. In preaching about the resurrection of Jesus, Paul awakened in his hearers an expectation and hope that the risen Christ would soon return. He assured them that his coming would not mean wrath and judgment but mercy and life everlasting. Such a faith transformed those who embraced it. It gave a new meaning to their lives and motivated them to change.

Paul recalls the real joy with which the Thessalonians embraced the gospel and its way of life. He reminds them how they committed themselves to imitate him as he himself had modeled his life on that of Jesus. What concretely that entails for Paul can be summed up in the word love. As Jesus loved us and gave himself for us, so are we to love one another.

Self-Forgetful Service

31ST SUNDAY IN ORDINARY TIME
Readings: Mal 1:14b–2:2b, 8-10, 1 Thess 2:7b-9, 13, Mt 23:1-12

Read in terms of its original context, today's gospel offers a dramatic contrast between the attitudes of the leaders of rabbinic Judaism and those that are to mark the community of Jesus' disciples. Our listening to it in the liturgy should focus not on the past but on how we can apply it to ourselves, how we can recognize, in what it condemns, our own failings, and, in what it recommends, the ideal that we ought to be pursuing.

People in positions of leadership and responsibility, whether in school or office, state or church, can easily be blinded by their own self-importance. They can become insensitive both to the difficulties and struggles of those under them and to their own inadequacies. Jesus' comment about how they love to have places of honor and receive public recognition rings as true today as when he first said it.

The fundamental concern of such people is not to be of service and help to others but to further their own reputations and careers. What ultimately motivates them is a form of self-seeking. They revel in and want to enhance if possible the power and prestige that their position gives them.

A Community of Mutual Service

All of this, Jesus says, is quite at odds with what it is to be his disciple. The Christian community should be marked by a sense of radical equality and shared dignity. We are all sisters and brothers, children of a single Father. We all exist under one authority, that of God and of Christ.

Those who are great, Jesus says, those who by nature or

grace have something to offer to others, are to put their gifts at the service of the community. If taken literally, what Jesus says about calling no one father or teacher does not correspond to our experience in the church or in the world. The intent behind the saying, however, goes beyond mere words. Authority, whether of position or of talent, means service. It has nothing to do with domination or self-seeking.

The theme of mutual service is so central to the gospel that it must be seen as one of its distinguishing features. Other texts, including those of the last supper, emphasize that the model that we are to imitate here is Jesus himself.

To Share Our Own Selves

Today's second reading shows how the gospel teaching about service was understood and lived by one of the great leaders and authorities of the early church. Paul was acutely conscious of his role and responsibility as an apostle. He preached the gospel with conviction and forcefulness and did not hesitate to confront and disagree with those who, in his judgment, were distorting it or impeding its spread.

In the present text Paul reminds the Thessalonians of the tenderness and gentleness with which he had come among them. He worked with his hands in order not to be a burden to them. In everything he did he was motivated by the double desire of serving the gospel and of serving them.

In spite of all the good priests, religious and lay people who over the years have served the Catholic community in various forms of leadership, we cannot but be aware today of how often others have failed in their responsibilities. The church has suffered grievously from the hypocrisy, the arrogance, the insensitivity and worse of too many of its leaders.

Corrupting the Covenant

Today's first reading from Malachi evokes a theme that comes back repeatedly throughout the prophetic books of the Bible. Through the prophet God confronts the priests with their failures, warns them of the consequences of what they are doing, and calls them to repentance.

In today's text, as in many others, the priests are upbraided for their lack of knowledge of God and of God's ways, and for the inadequacy of their teaching. They have become corrupted and in turn have corrupted those whom they are called to lead. They have broken the covenant, that solemn mutual commitment with God that lies at the basis of their priestly office.

Christian leadership in its different forms is today passing through a very difficult period. The present crisis has many causes, some of which are more cultural than religious. The renewal of ordained and non-ordained forms of leadership, so sorely needed, will only come about if we can rediscover and begin to embody in our most fundamental attitudes the ideal of servant leadership lived and taught by Jesus.

Christ's Coming in Glory

32ND SUNDAY IN ORDINARY TIME
Readings: Wis 6:12-16, 1 Thess 4:13-18, Mt 25:1-13

Both the gospel and the second reading of today's liturgy speak of the return or second coming of Christ at the end of time. The parable of the ten virgins or bridesmaids evokes it within the context of a warning. The Lord, it says, may come at any moment including when we least expect him. The challenge we face is to be ready to greet him whatever the time of his coming.

We are told that of the ten bridesmaids five were wise and five foolish. The wise ones had thought about, and had prepared for, the possibility that the bridegroom might be delayed. They brought extra oil so that no matter how long they had to wait they would be ready to meet him. The foolish, however, assumed that he would come right away, and when he did not, they had nothing to light their way.

Paul's letter to the Thessalonians reveals just how intensely many of the first Christians believed that the end times were at hand. The experience of the resurrection of Jesus was still very much alive for them and they thought of it as a sign that his return in glory would soon take place.

To Be with Christ Forever

The fact that some members of the community had died before the second coming created confusion and anxiety. People wondered what the fate of the dead would be when Christ did come. Paul assures them that all who have died in Christ will be brought to life in him. In this respect there will be no difference between the fate of those who have died and of those who are still alive.

In evoking the last days, Paul uses traditional apocalyptic

imagery. There will be a sound of trumpets and a call of angels and the coming of Christ on the clouds of heaven. The heart of Paul's message, however, goes beyond such images. We are to think of our dead and of ourselves not as people without hope but as those who believe that "we will be with the Lord forever."

For centuries most Christians have tended to relate what the New Testament says about the end times to their own death. Paradoxically, our own skeptical age with its nuclear weapons and its growing awareness of ecological destruction is haunted by apocalyptic fears and concerns. Now as always we need to hear Paul's message of hope and trust.

To Seek and To Love Wisdom

In the parable Jesus describes those bridesmaids who are thoughtful enough to bring along extra oil as wise. The word points to a theme that is central to the Bible, one which is associated in a special way with the life and mission of Jesus.

Today's first reading is from the book of Wisdom, one of several books in the Old Testament grouped together under the heading "wisdom literature." In these books, wisdom is often personified as a female figure actively involved with God in creation and in God's saving work among the people of Israel. In a famous phrase, wisdom is described as delighting to dwell among human beings, making of them friends of God.

Our reading emphasizes the beauty and radiance of wisdom. She offers those who seek her understanding and insight both about themselves and about God and God's ways. In the New Testament in general Jesus is presented as a teacher of wisdom and in John's gospel is hailed as wisdom incarnate.

The Wisdom of Life

Ours is a culture that puts a considerable premium on science and technology. Due to their rapid development our century has witnessed a knowledge explosion. Computers and other electronic instruments are making information and data available to us at an unprecedented rate. Never before have so many people had such easy access to so much knowledge.

In spite of our growing knowledge, however, and in spite too of all the good things that such knowledge has brought, as a culture we are faced with daunting problems on both the personal and the social levels. If human relations for many people are more difficult than ever, there is also a widespread public cynicism about institutions and about political life.

Wisdom is not the same thing as scientific or technical knowledge. It is both simpler and more profound. It has to do with who we are as moral and spiritual beings. Wisdom can help us discern values and make judgments about the things that really matter. Family and family relations, to take but one example, demand wisdom if they are to flourish. So too does political and social life. Wisdom can be pursued and fostered. It is also something for which we can pray. It remains a gift of God.

Responsible Activity

33RD SUNDAY IN ORDINARY TIME
**Readings: Prov 31:10-13, 16-18, 20, 26, 28-31,
1 Thess 5:1-6, Mt 24:36; 25:14-30**

The parable in today's gospel has to do with the return of Christ at the end of time and with the judgment that his coming will entail. The focus is on how we are to act in the interim, on what we are to do here and now so that when he comes we will be able to meet him with a sense of hope and expectation.

For the original readers of Matthew the word "talent" did not suggest abilities or gifts as it does for us but rather a relatively large sum of money. In the parable a man divides his holdings into amounts of differing size and entrusts them to three of his slaves according to their abilities. By shrewd investment two of them are able to double what was left them while the third, paralyzed by fear that he might lose what had been entrusted to him, buries it and produces no profit.

When the master returns he praises and rewards those slaves who have been creative and productive and condemns the one who did nothing. He accuses him of laziness and wickedness and has him cast out of the household into the outer darkness.

Using Our Talents

Whatever the original meaning of the word talent, it is easy to understand how on the basis of today's parable it came to take on the meaning that it now has. The point of the story is clearly not about investing money but rather about using in a creative and responsible way the gifts and abilities, the talents, that God has bestowed on us.

The parable speaks to us both as individuals and as members of various communities, civic and national as well as ecclesial.

197

Life at all its levels has been given to us not just for safekeeping but for development. The story of creation, for example, speaks of human stewardship for the world. The church, for its part, has been entrusted with the message of the gospel and the gift of Christ's Spirit so that it can bring them into fruitful interaction with all peoples and with the whole of human history.

Our God is a living God, a God of life who calls us forward into life. To be alive is to grow and develop and to contribute to the well-being of our families and of all of humanity. We have different abilities, different gifts; what we all have in common is the responsibility to develop them and to put them at the service of the larger community.

A Good Woman, Strong and Gentle

Today's first reading, taken from the book of Proverbs, offers a striking example of a person who clearly used her gifts. The passage contains an eloquent hymn extolling the virtues of a strong and energetic, active and creative woman. She nurtures her family and contributes to the well-being of society. She is particularly sensitive to the poor and the needy.

In earlier chapters of Proverbs divine wisdom is portrayed as a woman. Active with God in creation and present in the world teaching and guiding people in the ways of goodness and righteousness, Lady Wisdom personifies the nurturing closeness of God to human life. If a female figure is able to evoke such divine qualities, it seems only fitting that the example the book gives of a human life responding to and embodying the gift of wisdom should be that of a woman. She both acts wisely and is a teacher of wisdom. She renders concrete the ideal that we are all invited to pursue.

Children of Light

In today's second reading Paul once again talks about the end of time. No one, he says, knows when Christ will return. His coming will be sudden and unexpected, but that should make no difference to believers. They are children of light and of the day and as such ought always to be awake and ready.

Although very few of us have any sense of an impending end of the world, there is something about the attitude suggested by today's readings that should be a part of every Christian life. To believe in God as revealed in Jesus Christ is to believe in a God who calls us by name, who cares for and is interested in us and in our well-being. He respects our freedom and encourages our sense of responsibility.

We have all been given a variety of gifts. Some are rooted in nature; others have come to us through the social, economic and political situations into which we have been born. As believers we have been gifted in a special way with God's Spirit. Whatever our gifts, we should think of them as things for which one day we will have to give an account. Let us not be fearful or lazy but rather creative and generous in our use of them.

God All in All

34TH SUNDAY IN ORDINARY TIME — CHRIST THE KING
Readings: Ezek 34:11-12, 15-17, 1 Cor 15:20-26, 28, Mt 25:31-46

The last Sunday of the liturgical year is also the feast of Christ the King. The readings emphasize the end times and the final triumph of Christ and our sharing in it. The gospel this year contains Matthew's majestic and challenging account of the coming in glory of the Son of Man and of the judgment on all peoples and nations over which he will preside.

Jesus begins his description of that final event by comparing his role in it to that of a shepherd separating sheep from goats. The same image occurs in today's first reading where Ezekiel uses it to describe God's relation to Israel. God, he says, is like a shepherd who cares about and seeks out his flock, especially those who are lost or weak. But, the prophet continues, God will also judge between one sheep and another. The graciousness of God is not incompatible with and even calls out for a judgment. Ezekiel here looks forward to one of the paradoxes of the gospel. If it is good news in its proclamation of God's forgiveness and love, it also includes a judgment. In a strange way this too is good news; without it, our freedom and responsibility would lose much of their significance.

To Serve Those in Need

What Jesus stresses in his account of the judgment is the norm or criterion by which our lives are to be measured. As well known as the text is, it merits being pondered again and again. In the end we will be judged primarily not on our knowledge or success or even our religious practice but rather on the way we have treated those who hunger and thirst, those who lack clothes and shelter, those who are sick or in prison.

The list Jesus gives here of human needs is in no sense exhaustive. It suggests in a concrete way the kind of things that are implied in the gospel teaching on love of neighbor. What Jesus asks of us is that we be good to one another and especially to those who are in need. Love in his mind has nothing to do with sentimentality. It demands practical action that changes the situation of those to whom we reach out. This obviously applies not only to strangers but also and especially to our children, spouses, elderly parents, friends and neighbors. We will be judged not on vague and general feelings, but on what we actually did or did not do for specific individuals.

You Did It to Me

One of the more striking features in Jesus' account of the final judgment is his claim that what we do or fail to do for people in need is in fact done or not done to him. Jesus clearly identifies himself with all the categories of needy people that he evokes. This is something, he says, that at the end will come as an enormous surprise both to those who have reached out to others and to those who have failed to do so.

Some scholars have suggested that the mention here of Jesus' sisters and brothers refers in a special way to his disciples. As true to some degree as this may be, it is difficult to imagine that the text only refers to them. In entering into a human life in Jesus, the Son of God drew near to and in some way identified with all human beings. Over the centuries this conviction has stimulated untold numbers of Christians to embrace and help the abandoned and the downtrodden.

Made Alive in Christ

The proclamation of the story of the judgment in the liturgy should not be seen simply as a warning about a future event but rather as a pressing and present invitation. It challenges us here and now to think about the kind of people we are and the way

202 PREPARING FOR WORSHIP

we act. Do we recognize in one another the face of Christ? Do we allow ourselves to be touched by need?

In today's second reading Paul speaks of the end in terms of final fulfillment. As children of Adam we are destined to die, but as brothers and sisters of Christ we are called to eternal life. The resurrection of Jesus is the promise and the beginning of the resurrection to which we are all called.

Paul sees human history as a time of gradual triumph for Christ. When finally all things including death will be subject to him, he will hand them over to God so that God will be all in all. With Christ's resurrection, the end has already begun. We began to share in it with our baptism. Christian life involves an ever more profound immersion into the death and resurrection of Jesus. The more we live through the Spirit in Christ, the more God lives in us; the more God lives in us the more we can experience even now a foretaste of eternal life.

Assumption, All Saints, and Immaculate Conception

Death Will Be Destroyed

AUGUST 15 — THE ASSUMPTION OF MARY
Readings: Rev 11:19a; 12:1-6a, 10ab, 1 Cor 15:20-26, Lk 1:39-56

At times in Christian history salvation has been understood more in relation to the next life and at other times more in relation to this one. In the early church there was an acute sense that the world was near its end and that the risen Christ would soon return to save his followers from the coming judgment. Later the emphasis was put on the death of the individual. The Christian hope became predominantly a hope for eternal life with God in heaven. In our own day there has been an increasing concern with what salvation means for the here and now. We try to understand its relation to contemporary struggles for peace, justice and a renewed human relationship with the environment.

The feast of the assumption of Mary emphasizes ultimate fulfillment in Christ, but it does so in such a way as to underline the importance of our existence in the world. Today's second reading is from a longer passage in which Paul passionately defends faith in the resurrection of Jesus. For him Christianity stands or falls with Christ's resurrection. It is both a saving event in itself and a revelation of our final destiny. The risen Christ is the first-born of many sisters and brothers.

Made Alive in Christ

Explicit faith in the assumption of Mary is something that was unknown in the first several centuries of the church's history. It seems to have developed through a deepening reflection on the importance of Mary's involvement in God's plan of salvation and a growing conviction that the salvation meant for all of us was brought to its first and richest expression in her.

If Paul emphasizes that in Christ we can hope for a life beyond this one, he also makes clear that this new life is not restricted to the spiritual element in us but includes our bodily existence as well. At the heart of Christian faith is the affirmation that the Word or Son of God entered into and embraced a full human life in the person of Jesus. Our religion is radically incarnational. It takes the material world and the body seriously and includes both in its view of future fulfillment. The resurrection of Jesus marks his going home to God in the fullness of his embodied existence. The dogma of the assumption of Mary affirms that from the instant of her death she shared in that total salvation for which we all hope.

New Heavens and New Earth

Today's reading from the book of Revelation describes a dramatic and symbolic vision of a confrontation between two remarkable figures. The one is a majestic heavenly woman and the other a monstrous and destructive dragon. She gives birth to a child which the animal seeks to devour but which God saves.

The woman probably refers to Israel giving birth to the messiah and to the church threatened by persecution and destruction and yet protected by God until the end times. The dragon is identified with the serpent of Genesis and with Satan, the adversary of God and of all that is good. Later Christian tradition came to regard the woman as Mary and to see in her heavenly state an indication of her fulfillment in God.

The text suggests the all-embracing character of Christian salvation. The struggle between good and evil is played out in heaven and on earth and will only be resolved by that final transformation of all things hinted at by the concluding hymn.

She Who Believed

The basic affirmation of Christian faith in regard to Mary is that she is the mother of Jesus, the mother of the Word incarnate.

Today's gospel reminds us that her involvement in this role was the result of a conscious and free choice on her part. Elizabeth proclaims her blessed because she believed that God would indeed bring about what he had promised.

Mary's response to Elizabeth's greeting is the only possible human reaction to God's saving grace. In spite of all we do to be people of faith and to lead lives of love and hope, salvation comes from God. All generations call Mary blessed not primarily for what she has done but rather for what God has brought about in and through her. This is always part of our celebration of Mary and her role in the life and destiny of Jesus.

The fact that Mary has been brought to fulfillment in her embodied existence tells us something essential about our destiny and that of all of creation. Salvation involves the whole person and in some sense the cosmos itself. What we do here and now to make that salvation a present reality will not be lost but rather taken up in our final transformation in God.

Called To Be Saints

NOVEMBER 1 — ALL SAINTS
Readings: Rev 7:2-4, 9-14, 1 Jn 3:1-3, Mt 5:1-12a

Since the ninth century the liturgical year has included a special day honoring and celebrating all those holy women and men otherwise unknown who have lived the mystery of grace to its fullness and who have been brought to eternal life in God. Such a day celebrates something central to Christianity. Our profession in the creed of the holiness of the church is an affirmation not only about the presence of the Holy Spirit in word, gift, and sacrament, but also about the Spirit's effectiveness in transforming the lives of ordinary believers.

Today's first reading is from the book of Revelation's symbolic and dramatic portrayal of the heavenly world and of the unfolding of the end times. The true servants of God are to be marked by an identifying sign in order not that they will escape death but that in and through it they will be brought to final salvation. The number of those to be sealed is symbolic. While some are from the tribes of Israel, the majority represent the many nations and languages of the earth. They will stand before God robed in white and carrying symbols of victory. Washed in baptism, they have been made strong by the blood of the Lamb.

Blessing and Glory to God

What we are given in the text is an imaginative vision of the heavenly liturgy. The redeemed cry out in word and song, praising and blessing God and giving thanks for their salvation. Their prayer underlines just how much holiness is more than simply living a moral life. It has to do with God and begins and ends with God's grace.

Today's second reading makes the same point in slightly

different language. It points to the mystery of God's love. It is because God loves us that he shares the divine life with us, making us in name and in fact children of God. Here is a theme that is central to the gospel as well as the letters of John. To be baptized in Christ is to be born to a new life.

John draws a connection between what we are in Christ and what we will become in the next life. Although the exact nature of our fulfillment in God has not been revealed, he is convinced that on the basis of faith we can be certain that we will be like God and see him as he is. This is the starting point for the later Christian understanding of the beatific vision, a knowing of God that will fill us with happiness and peace.

To Purify Ourselves

If the emphasis in the first two readings is on what God does for us in our sanctification, there is also a strong sense that we have to cooperate with him. Those who were strengthened in Christ had to stand firm in the face of trial and persecution. John speaks of our need to purify ourselves so that we will be more like God and Christ.

The idea of purity here embraces more than sexuality. The word evokes the ritual purity that was so much a part of Jewish life. If one wanted to pray or enter into the presence of God in the temple one had to be purified of everything that stood in contradiction to God. For Jesus this involves above all an ethical and religious state of soul. One has to be free of anger and hatred and self-seeking. Put positively, purity of heart demands forgiveness, mercy and love. What more specifically it entails can be found in the gospels and especially in the sermon on the mount.

Living the Beatitudes

The qualities and attitudes praised in the beatitudes have long been seen as central to the moral and religious ideal that Jesus preached. They are the kind of things that one would expect to find in people seriously living the Christian life.

The profile of the saint is quite different from that of the powerful but flawed figure of the ancient hero. Saints are aware of their limitations and of their need for God's help. This is why Jesus begins the beatitudes by mentioning the poor in spirit, the meek, and those who mourn. Such people know about the brokenness and brittleness of human life and therefore about their dependence on God's healing and strengthening presence.

And yet saints are not passive. They hunger and thirst for justice, exercise mercy, and do what they can to bring about peace and reconciliation in the world around them. Everything they do is based on faith in God and Christ and on the values they have imbibed from the gospels. Our celebration of such people should be an occasion for us to renew our own religious and moral commitment. May their prayers help us to do so.

Chosen by God

DECEMBER 8 — THE IMMACULATE CONCEPTION
Readings: Gen 3:9-15, 20, Eph 1:3-6, 11-12, Lk 1:26-38

Although the dogma of the immaculate conception was only formally defined in 1854, the truth about Mary to which it points was a focus of prayer and devotion among Christians from a very early date. As with so much of Catholic teaching about Mary it grew up as a result of meditation on her unique role in the story of salvation. She was called to be the mother of the Word incarnate, the woman in whom the Son of God took on flesh.

Today's feast celebrates a reality that is central to Mary's identity as a spiritual person. It is concerned with the nature of her relationship to God from the first instance of her existence. St. Paul and then St. Augustine and others after him reflected at great length on the universality of sin and on the depth of the alienation from God to which it pointed. Eventually their convictions about all this came to be articulated in the doctrine of original sin. Human beings, the doctrine affirms, were made to live in harmony with God, with one another and with all of creation. The sins of humanity, however, beginning with the sin of the first humans, undermined this ideal and introduced conflict and tension with God and with one another into the heart of human experience.

Sin and Hope

Today's first reading evokes the biblical account of the sin of Adam and Eve and especially of its disastrous consequences. The harmony that had existed between the couple and God has been undermined. Adam hides from God, and when confronted with what he has done, he turns on his wife. She in turn blames her failing on the serpent and its false promises.

Although the book of Genesis speaks of specific punishments for both the man and the woman, our reading focuses on the curse that God lays on the serpent. Later tradition identified the serpent with Satan and saw in the prediction of a conflict between his offspring and the offspring of the woman a veiled allusion to a future redeemer. Christians came to cherish these verses as a "proto" or first gospel. They related its good news to Jesus and interpreted its mention of "the woman" as a reference to Mary. She is the new Eve, the new mother of the living, the one who will give birth to the messiah whose destiny it is to communicate a new and renewed life to all who believe in him.

The Servant of the Lord

The role and attitude of Mary in the story of salvation is brought out most compellingly in Luke's treatment of the conception and birth of Jesus. Today's gospel contains his well-known account of the annunciation. Salvation begins with God. It is God who sends his Son and who through the Son's human life, death and resurrection offers forgiveness and reconciliation. As much as the scriptures emphasize God's activity, they also insist on our collaboration with it. This is the meaning of the incarnation. Jesus is both divine and human. In him a human being freely and lovingly collaborates with God in effecting salvation.

The principle of the incarnation extends beyond Jesus to embrace both Mary and the church. The story of the annunciation affirms not only that Jesus was born of Mary but that she was a conscious and free participant in the process. By her faith and loving response she became an active partner with God in all that he was to do for us in Christ.

To the Praise of God's Glory

Today's second reading contains part of the prayer of praise and blessing that begins the letter to the Ephesians. It pushes the story of salvation back beyond the time not only of Jesus but also of Moses and Abraham and even of humanity itself. God chose us in Christ before the foundation of the world. He chose us to share his life here and now through faith and love and to be gifted in the end with every spiritual blessing.

It was texts like this one that helped believers to understand how Mary had escaped the alienation from God that is a part of every human life without that gift in any way undermining the universality of Christ's saving work. They recognized that anything that Mary received was related to and dependent on the salvation that was yet to come but which had been destined from all eternity by God.

Our celebration of today's feast reminds us of the reality of sin and alienation but also of the even greater reality of God's saving purpose in Christ and of Mary's role in it. For all this we give thanks. Like Mary, we too are called to live the kind of life that gives praise and glory to God.